The life & times of the 2CV

The life & times of the 2CV

Bob MacQueen
Julian McNamara

Great Ouse Press

© Bob MacQueen and Julian McNamara 1982

All rights reserved. No part of this publication may be reproduced or transmitted, in any form or by any means, without permission.

First published 1982 by
GREAT OUSE PRESS LTD

Great Ouse Press
82 Castle Street, Cambridge CB3 0AJ
Telephone Cambridge (0223) 521030

ISBN 0-907351-07-7

This book is sold subject to the condition that it shall not, by way of trade or otherwise, be lent, resold, hired out, or otherwise circulated without the publisher's prior consent in any form of binding or cover other than that in which it is published and without a similar condition including this condition being imposed on the subsequent purchaser.

Designed by Art-Work-Shop

Printed in Great Britain by Butler and Tanner.

ACKNOWLEDGEMENTS

The authors extend their grateful thanks to all who have helped in the compilation of this book especially Fabien Sabates, Maurice Leroy, Julien Vlaminck, Peter Nunn, Tony Dron, Martin Jones, Ken Garrett, Marie-Hélène Poupet and Paul Bucket of Citroën, Ian Alcock, David Conway, David Lawrie, the Citroën Car Club and Cecil Aviation of Cambridge. Not forgetting Susie, Andy and Jim at Great Ouse Press. Also Tony Curtis of *Motor* for permission to reproduce the road test and show review and Huiles Yacco for page 97. And of course grateful thanks for all help and cooperation from SA Citroën France and Slough.

Contents

	Page
Prologue	8
1: Beginnings	10
2: The Development	16
3: The Debutante	26
4: The First Adventurers	42
5: The Plastic 2CVs	60
6: The Anglo Saxons & the 2CV	68
7: Cross Country 2CVs	78
8: Further Developments	94
9: Oddities	103
10: The Clubs	124

APPENDICES

1: A Brief Guide to Model Nomenclature for Post-War 2CVs	136
2: Buying a Used 2CV – some of the pitfalls	137
3: Technical Report by Ken Garrett in the Automobile Engineer	138
4: Some Citroën Literature	148
5: One Enthusiast's View	157

Prologue

'Une voiture pouvant transporter deux cultivateurs en sabots, cinquante kilos de pommes de terre ou un tonnelet'
Pierre-Jules Boulanger, President of Citroën 1935

Wednesday October 7th 1948

10 pm. In an interview with Charles Faroux, then France's premier motoring journalist, Pierre Boulanger denied categorically any intention on the part of the company to introduce their much rumoured 'people's car' at the following day's Paris Motor Show.

11 pm. Amid security precautions more normally reserved for heads of state three small shrouded cars made their appearance on the Citroën stand. "They were," observed one member of the press, "literally surrounded by senior personnel who forbade anyone to touch or even look, but it could be seen that the suspension was very soft...."

Thursday October 8th 1948

Having declared the Motor Show officially open the President of the French Republic, Vincent Auriol, began his series of courtesy visits to his country's major motor manufacturers gathered along the Grande Avenue. Amid mounting excitement on the Citroën stand Pierre Boulanger stepped forward to welcome him. It was the moment the crowds had been waiting for. As the two shook hands, with typically gallic panache the shrouds were lifted from the mystery cars. Flash bulbs exploded, onlookers stared bemused and Citroën had achieved a publicity coup.

The 2CV was born.

Opposite: *"Available for delivery in 1949 at 185,000 francs"* proclaimed the notices beside the cars. *"This small abortion in metallic grey"* proclaimed one Paris paper. The public however disagreed. (Citroën)

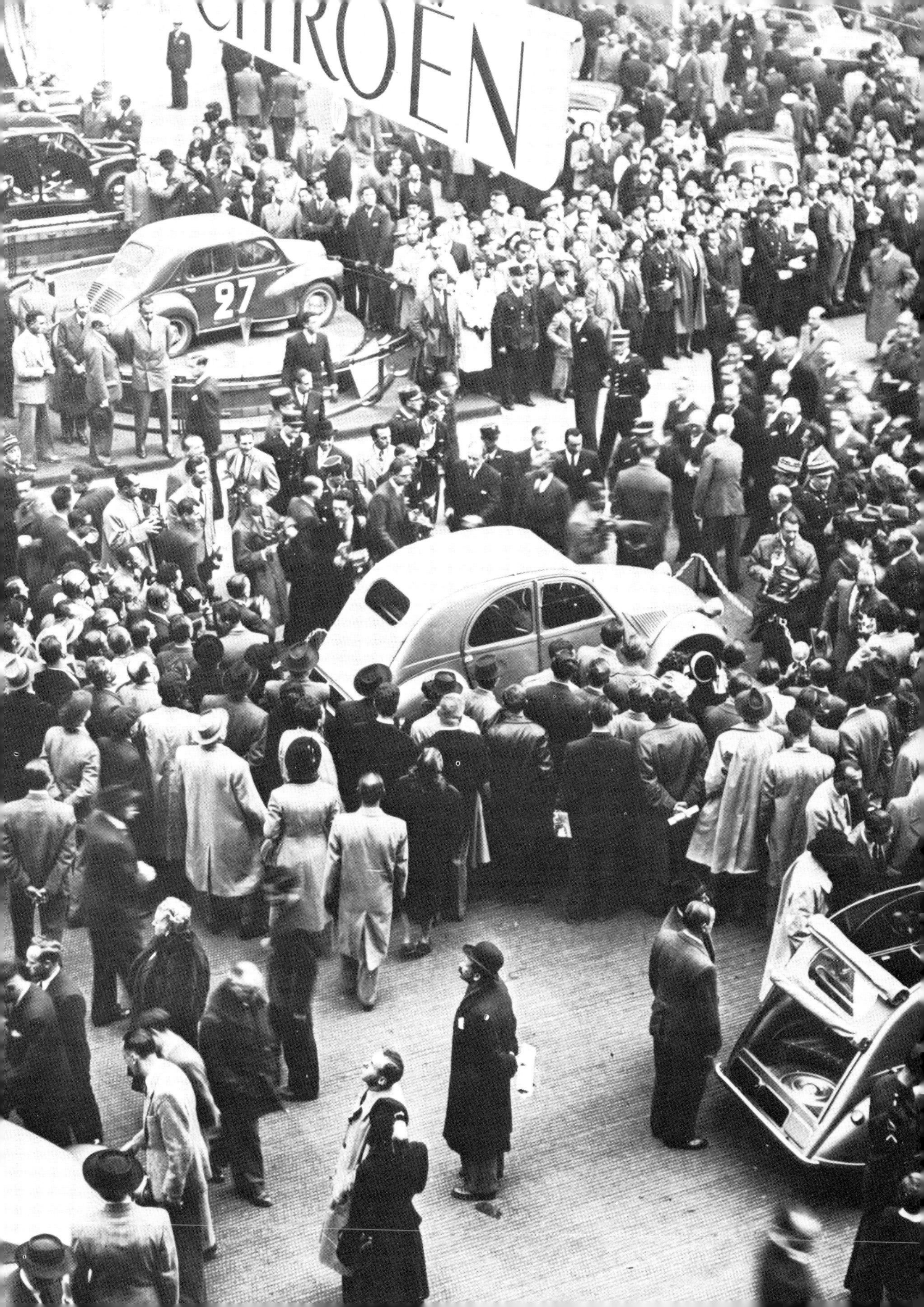
CITROËN
27

1 Beginnings

The concept of the 2CV lay rooted in the unhappy sequence of events which made 1934 a year of technical triumph and personal tragedy for André Citroën. The crippling development costs of the revolutionary *Traction Avant* aggravated by his policy of maintaining the highest industrial wages in Paris and compounded by the gradual decline in demand for the *Rosalie* 8CV were inexorably pushing the company which bore his name into receivership.

While the shares slipped to an all time low and industrial discontent gnawed at the fabric of the whole group, Citroën desperately sought to buy time. Creditors were prevailed upon to allow deferment after deferment while his own holding in the company was pledged to the Michelin family. Even as the magnificent banquets and special trains brought flocks of customers for the new car, France's greatest industrialist was beginning to succumb to a far more implacable foe than his creditors.

In 1933 it had been realised that the Javel plant could not possibly cope with the demands of the new production techniques needed for the *Traction*. Citroën's solution was totally in keeping with all his other acts, he tore down the factory and completely rebuilt it, reputedly without losing one day's production. The strain upon all concerned was intense but in Citroën's case it was to prove fatal. Unequal to fighting both ill health and his creditors he petitioned for bankruptcy. The government stepped in and control passed into the hands of the Michelin family whilst André Citroën took to his bed to leave it but briefly before his untimely death in 1935.

Ironically the car which caused the breakdown of the *patron* was to prove the salvation of the company. Once the early teething troubles were sorted out, the *Traction* went on to take the market by storm. That it was able to do so was due in large measure to Pierre Michelin who took the somewhat unusual step of persuading his company's architect to

Opposite: Boulanger (far right) with then current aerophotography camera. Inset – smoking the perennial cigarette in front of his own aircraft. (Citroën)

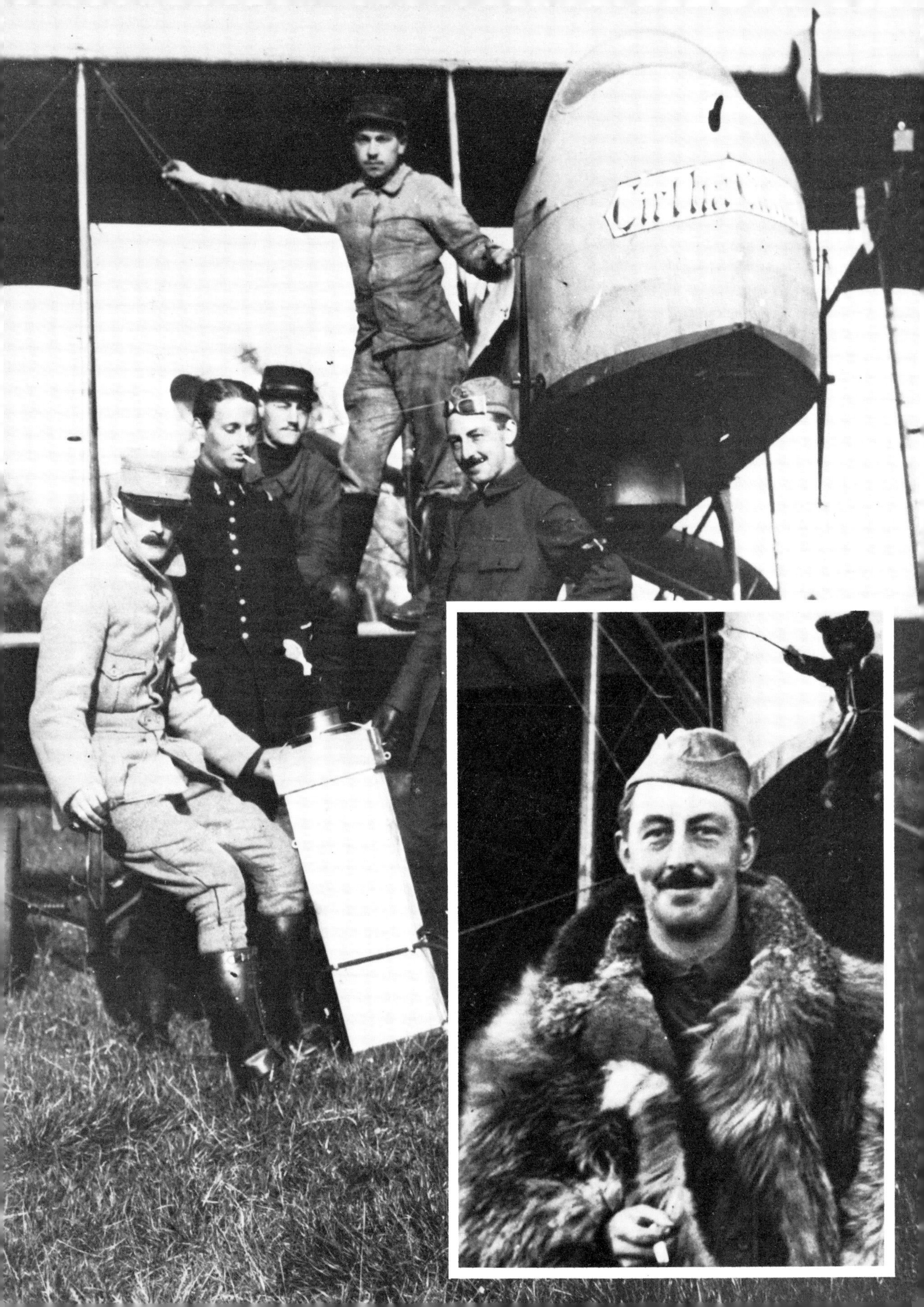

Above: The first official publicity photo of the Traction Avant. (Citroën)

accept the colossal task of restoring order to the staggering empire.

At first glance Pierre-Jules Boulanger (PJB to the staff) would seem a most unlikely candidate to fill the shoes of André Citroën. Contemporary reports describe him as an unassuming man in a grey suit and hat, swamped by an enormous raincoat, who habitually recorded his every thought in a succession of black covered pocket notebooks and was never seen without a cigarette.

His first contact with the Michelins had been in 1905 when he and Marcel served together during national service in the Observer Corps at Satory. In retrospect it now seems typical of the man that in an age when the middle classes reigned supreme and any adventure except in government or commercial service was frowned upon, he should at the end of his training decide to see something of the world.

With his sights set firmly upon the prosperity of the new world he joined with a party of friends in a trip to the States arriving at the beginning of 1908. Starting as a labourer, his travels took him gradually across the continent until in 1910 he secured a position as a draughtsman with a firm of architects in Seattle. A year passed before wanderlust once more took him in tow, this time to Canada, where he gradually established a thriving building business.

In 1914 the call to arms brought him back to France where his earlier training in aerophotography brought him a commission in the *Armée de l'Air* and eventual promotion to captain. The war also brought him back into contact with Marcel Michelin with the result that, on his demobilisation in 1919, Edouard Michelin approached him with the offer to supervise the construction of workers housing for the massive tyre company.

In the event Michelin could hardly have chosen a better saviour for Citroën. His quiet efficient way of assessing problems coupled with a considerateness and incisiveness in action soon restored confidence both within and outside the company. Indeed, so successful was he that by the close of 1935 the company, although no longer the single largest manufacturer in Europe, could begin to relax and face the future with a degree of confidence and the knowledge that almost all the company's debts had been discharged.

Into the calm of this idyllic situation Boulanger fired his remarkable salvo. Calling upon the then head of research and design, one M. Brogly, he calmly recited his famous specification for a people's car. The price, stated PJB, should be about half that of the 11CV. It should be capable of maintaining a steady 60kph, fully loaded, and return a consumption of not less than forty five miles per gallon. In conclusion he demanded that it should be capable of being driven across the roughest terrain by a learner driver in *"confort irréprochable"*.

Brogly decided he had heard enough. Confessing later that it was the most unreasonable specification he'd ever heard he began a catalogue of reasons why such a project could never succeed. Nevertheless PJB remained immovable. It could be done and it would be done. France, he pointed out, was experiencing sweeping social changes. The peasant had a right to his car and with the full blessing of the socially conscious Michelin family he fully intended that car to be a Citroën.

By the spring of 1936 the project was beginning to take shape. Working in the strictest secrecy under the code name TPV (for *Toute Petite Voiture*) Brogly assembled his team. The first priority, he decided, was to explore as fully as possible the potential market. With this in mind a conscientious and painstaking market survey was commissioned under the command of an engineer named Jacques Duclos.

Within five months the survey had covered the whole of France and ascertained the driving habits of some ten thousand potential customers. Piece by piece the nature of the vehicle needed to satisfy this market emerged. The average load, range and speed were assessed as were the practical equipment preferences of the potential operators.

However even before the final results of the survey had been collated the project had captured the imagination of the brilliant engineer André Lefebvre. To the man credited with finally solving the problem inherent in mass producing front wheel drive cars, the idea of a revolutionary people's car was irresistible.

Lefebvre had been a development engineer with Gabriel Voisin the pioneer aviator who had entered the car market with a stillborn project commissioned by André Citroën in 1917 for an 18CV tourer. As was the custom in those days, Lefebvre had also raced the cars he designed and his last project for Voisin had been a magnificent V12 front wheel drive car which had been killed by the economic climate. As Voisin slid into obscurity he had moved to Renault before being recruited by André Citroën in 1933. Not surprisingly he was a fervent believer in using aviation technology to solve automotive problems.

Taking Boulanger's specification he set to work. In the interests of overall economy he decided on a maximum weight limit for the new project of 300 kilogrammes and, in order to meet this, proposed a semi monocoque construction of duralumin using modified torsion bar suspension, relying upon Dr Junkers' method of corrugations to provide the necessary torsional stiffness.

The TPV was, from the beginning, a curious mixture of old and new ideas. André Citroën himself had been considering a smaller version of the *Traction* and Henri Forceau had already provided the basic design for the gear box and transmission. Jowett in Great Britain had been producing a flat-twin engined car with the radiator mounted above and behind the power plant in an almost unchanged format since 1911 and a first class light flat-twin engine was readily available as an interim measure in the form of the BMW 500 motorcycle engine. The idea of suspending the then current hammock type aircraft style seats from a bar in the roof and the use of magnesium castings to reinforce the duralumin structure were however very new.

As the results of the survey flooded in, the nucleus of the

design team assembled itself into some form of cohesion at the Bureau d'Etudes in the rue du Théâtre. From the team which had produced the *Traction* came Bertoni the stylist, Forceau the gear box wizard and Roger Prud'homme as head of research. To assist Bertoni a young man named Jean Murattet and to co-ordinate the project and maintain liaison with the factory Marcel Chinon was recruited from Amilcar.

Gradually it became apparent that the TPV was going to have to carry four passengers plus their luggage or equipment as a matter of course. Consequently Lefebvre modified his original concept to a platform chassis and with it began the gradual evolution of recognisable ancestors of the 2CV. Laboriously, after a great many false starts, the prototype took shape through the winter of 1936 until, in early spring 1937, Lefebvre agreed it was ready for testing.

Above: The factory at Javel (since named Quay André Citroën) before and after rebuilding in 1933. (Citroën)

2 The Development

Today, when the sound of a Citroën twin can be heard in almost every street in any European city, it is difficult to imagine the reaction of the more conservative elements of the company hierarchy to the failure of the first prototype. With its narrow track, lacking bodywork and fitted with a suspension hastily improvised from the *Traction*, the car which left the rue du Théâtre in 1937 was not so much a disappointment as a disaster. Even Lefebvre could manage only a few hundred metres behind its rudimentary perspex windscreen before resigning himself to another long session at the drawing board.

The place chosen for the first trials was Gometz-le-Chatel. Close enough to Paris to be convenient, it was reasoned, yet far enough distant that the press would be hard put to get wind of events. In the event the most interested body besides the designers and Boulanger was not the press but those at the factory who had kept alive André Citroën's idea for a smaller version of the *Traction*. Even as the post-mortems were being conducted the rival car was being readied for presentation to Boulanger.

To say that PJB was unimpressed with the usurper would be to understate the case. Taking the rival project as a direct condemnation of his policies, Boulanger quickly dismantled it, in the process giving ample proof that his placidity could be displaced by rare but towering rages. This done, his next act was to bring Sainturant, the designer of the ohv wet liner engine of the 11CV, into the TPV project, with instructions to provide a workable engine of the minimum required size and appropriate wear and torque characteristics. Meanwhile the rest of the team were set to work trying to make the car handle more in the fashion of motor vehicle than an unbroken mule.

Realising that further abortive public testing of the car could be embarrassing, Boulanger gave orders that a secret testing track was to be found. The ideal place, he directed, should be within a one hundred kilometer radius of Paris

Opposite: A rare photograph, which somehow evaded Boulanger's total ban, of three early prototypes at Ferté-Vidame in 1938. The lack of both radiator and filler cap on the left hand example suggest that it may be air cooled. (Fabien Sabates)

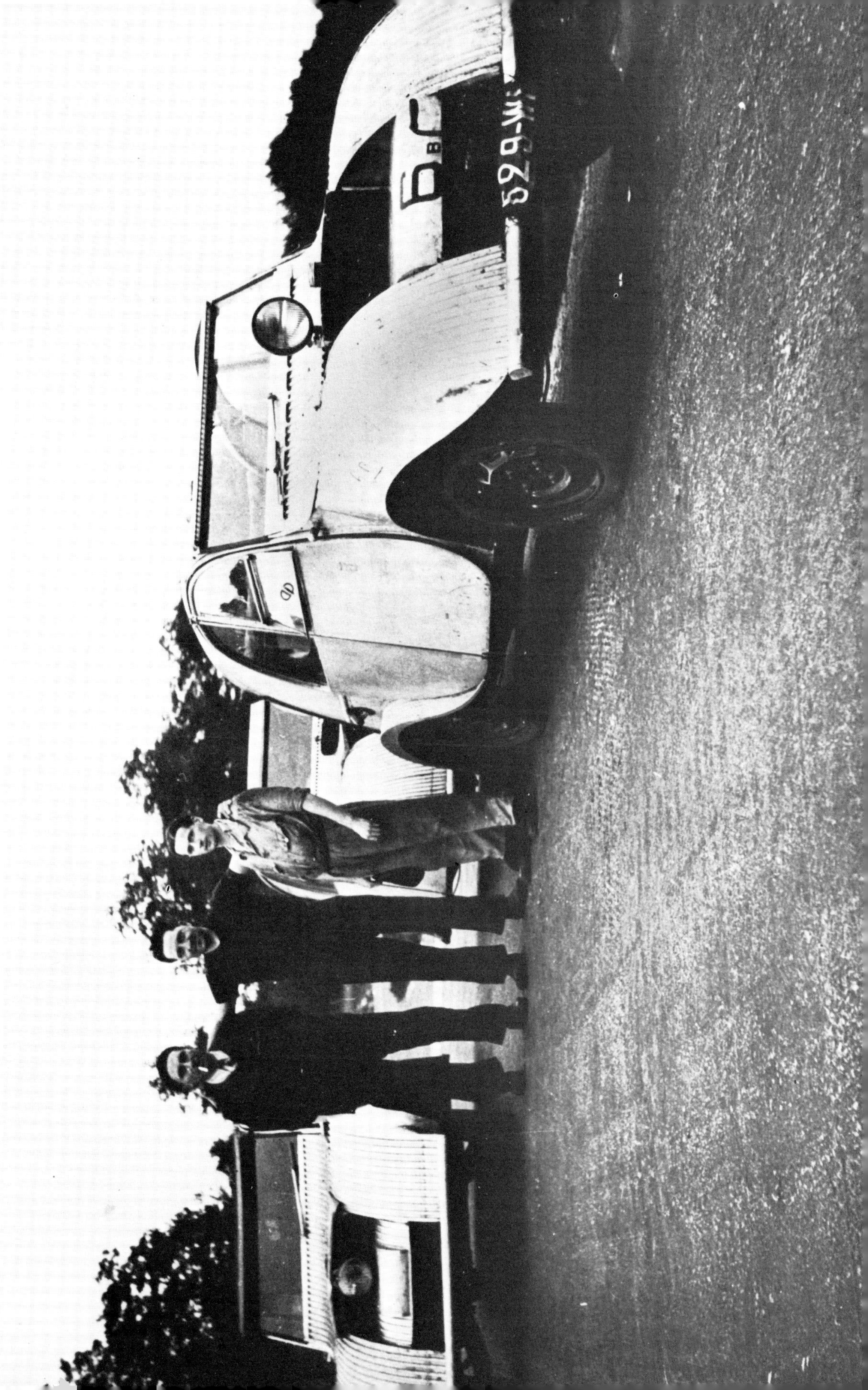

and preferably towards the west thus obviating the necessity of traversing the capital every time a new project needed to be delivered or reclaimed. The place chosen was a run down hunting park at Ferté-Vidame, Boulanger himself supervising the construction of the test track.

Here, during the winter of 1937, relying heavily on rum and coffee to keep themselves from freezing, a team of engineers began testing the stream of pre-series prototypes emanating from the rue du Théâtre. As well as the cold the test drivers had to contend with the inflammatory combination of aluminium, petrol and magnesium with the result that at least one of the pre-production cars ended its life in a spectacular blaze well before its appointed date for destruction.

During this period the cars really justified PJB's directive to build a vehicle comprising "four wheels, a platform and an umbrella." Often even the umbrella was missing as Bertoni struggled to keep pace with the changes wrought in the engine and suspension geometry. Still the testing went on until in May 1938 Boulanger was satisfied with the overall viability of the project and issued a directive that 250 prototypes were to be prepared for the following year's *Salon*.

Opposite and this page: The 1938 prototype in its definitive Salon form. This particular car was discovered by Jacques Wolgensinger in a barn at the testing track at Ferté-Vidame and subsequently rebuilt by Citroën with parts which had survived the mass scrapping. It was first shown to the public at the 1973 Le Mans 24 hours where it caused a sensation. Note the starting handle reputedly adopted in preference to a cord pull because the cord tended to break the nails of the secretaries at the rue du Théâtre. The single headlamp was all that legislation then demanded. The side and rear views demonstrate just how far advanced the concept of the cars for the Salon was. Note the studded wheels, lack of exterior door handles and the lack of visible evidence for the self levelling suspension. Following racing practice of the time the chassis has been drilled in the interests of saving weight. (Citroën)

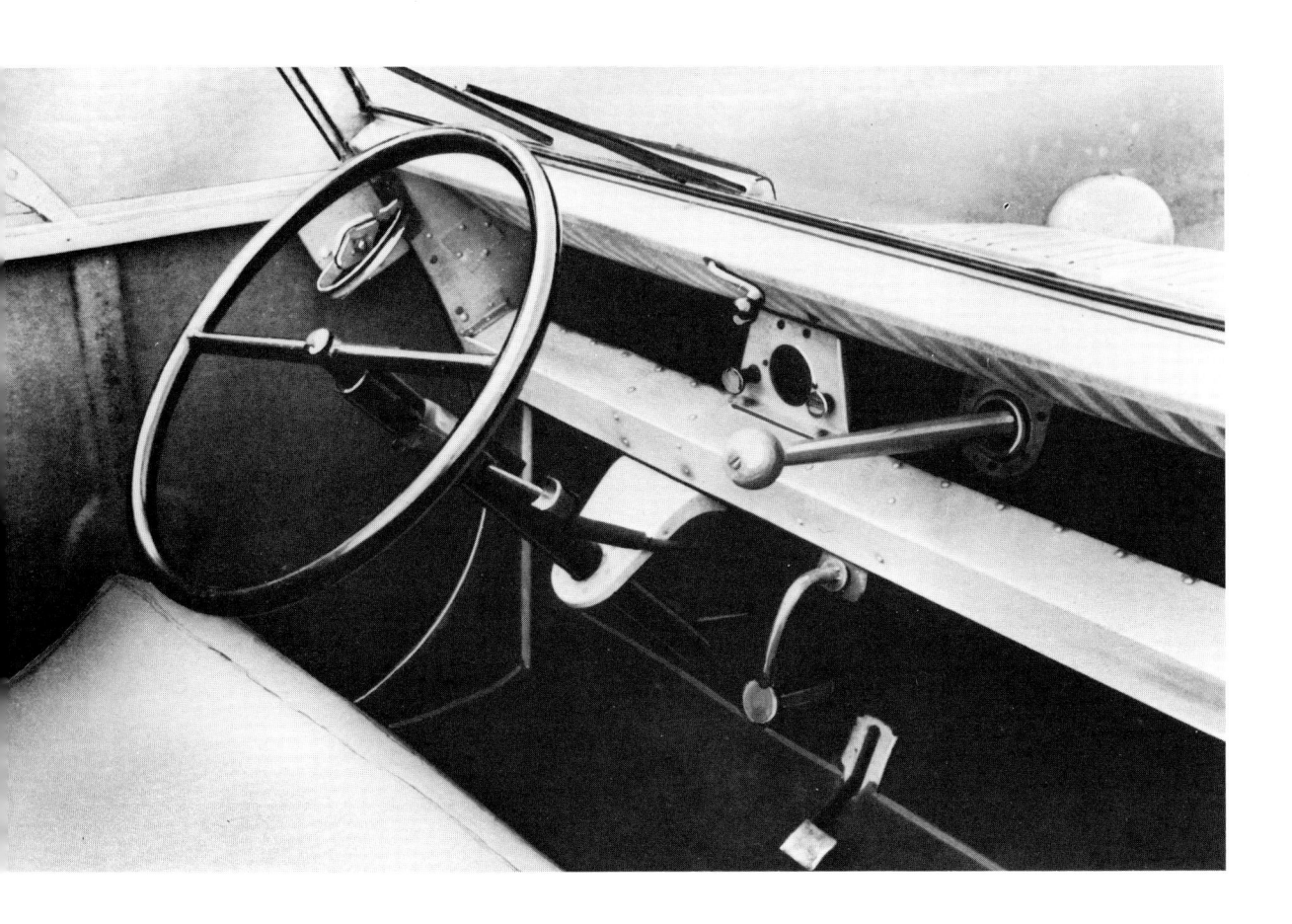

Above and left: Heavily retouched views of the interior plainly show the stark simplicity of the original dashboard with its hand operated wiper, lack of speedometer, column mounted lightswitch from the Traction and ammeter. The lower photo gives a fine view of the hammock seats whilst below the rear seat cushion the housing for the rear torsion bars can be seen. Note also the straight gear lever and primitive door handles. (Citroën)

Above and left: Two views of the watercooled engine showing the easy accessibility for owner servicing. (Citroën)

Ironically this directive was to be, at least in part, responsible for much of the confusion which surrounds the number and type of the pre-war prototypes. The need to build so many cars in the time allocated meant that the methods of production used for the pre-series cars would no longer suffice. In order to rationalise man hours the latest type of aluminium welding machines were needed. Of the types then available only the AEG machines were considered suitable and due to their strategic importance the sale of these machines was strictly controlled by Goering. Knowing the location of these machines was in effect, tantamount to knowing where aircraft fabrication could be taking place. This, in turn, explains the Luftwaffe's preoccupation in the early months of 1940 with flattening the Citroën factories with the consequent loss of most of the records of the car's development. Luckily, however a few important documents survived which help to chart the progress Lefebvre was making. One is the report on prototype number 34 which Jacques Borgé and Nicolas Viasnoff reproduced in full in *La 1CV*. This report lists some fifty good or bad points on this car and from it some interesting facts emerge.

As regards the engine, criticism was levelled at the twin carburettors, the right hand one being particularly difficult to service. The gear box oil was almost completely inaccessible. The engine oil was easily checked and replenished but the drain point was only easily available to someone with access to ramps or a pit. Draining the radiator and block was described as impractical whilst the jacking points were inadequate and the grease nipples had not yet been standardised.

The bodywork drew criticism for having no map pockets, for the lack of easy access to the driver's seat *"pour un usager assez grand"*, for insufficient ventilation and for the fact that the windscreen was not watertight. Other areas which drew unfavourable comment were the door handles and the roof; the former for their tendency to become detached the latter for its difficulty in doing so. The heating was insufficient, except where it fried the driver's feet, and the bulb for the single headlight was difficult to change.

Other faults catalogued were that the windscreen wiper left marks on the perspex windscreen, the gear lever did not fall easily to hand, the fuel tank was not large enough (5 litres) and was difficult to fill, and a short driver would need a cushion to see the road properly.

On the credit side the accessibility of the passenger seats

was praised as was the starting handle (previous prototypes were started by a cord). The petrol filler was protected from the rain and the depth of petrol and engine oil were easily accessible as were the ten greasing points. The exterior door handles had remained in place and the bonnet did a fine job in protecting the engine (a cryptic note here adds "unlike No.22").

The report describes the suspension as *"excellente"* which poses something of a mystery for if No.34 (christened *La Chouchoute*) was, as has occasionally been suggested the definitive model for the *Salon* car of 1939, it was still running with the original unsatisfactory torsion bar and swing arm of the earliest prototype even though Marcel Chinon had already evolved the self levelling interactive suspension from Mercier's original patents. The possibility remains that the cars destined for the *Salon* were for show as a design exercise whilst the further two hundred and fifty would be amended to take the fully revised suspension before being used in a great advance educational campaign for the dealers. Unfortunately as no definitive chassis plans of the later prototypes have survived and no coherent marketing schedule has come to light, the only substantiated statement on the change in suspension is that it had already taken place by the time Jean Cadiou took over as head of the Bureau d'Etudes in 1943 and was a reality by 1942 when Marcel Chinon was photographed driving a thus equipped prototype at Ferté-Vidame.

By May 1939 the engineers had reached number forty three in the table of prototype evolution. Most of the small details singled out for criticism in the earlier report had been successfully amended and the factory at Levallois was beginning to assemble the first of the 250 cars ordered for the *Salon*. Boulanger was already seeking Michelin support for yet another series batch, this time of five hundred cars to be fabricated completely at Levallois instead of various operations being spread through the factories of the whole group. The press had been primed with enticing hints that a sensational new car was on its way; all seemed set fair. But events beyond Boulanger's control were about to upset the coming of the new infant.

As the completed *Salon* cars began to be assembled in small groups at Levallois, France mobilised and brought the curtain down on the project. Three pre-series prototypes were quickly converted to small trucks and despatched to sit out the war as factory hacks at the Michelin works in Clermont-Ferrand. A few of the more complete examples of six *Salon* cars were secreted at Ferté-Vidame whilst the uncompleted bulk, plus the earlier prototypes, were ordered to be scrapped.[1]

As an early and staunch supporter of de Gaulle Boulanger found the German occupation totally unacceptable. Unlike some other French industrialists he set himself firmly to the task of making life as difficult as possible to the invaders with the inevitable result that his name quickly featured in the infamous Gestapo blacklist of influential Frenchmen who should be deported.

One of the manifestations of his hatred was a neurotic obsession, amply documented in his little black notebooks, with keeping the TPV out of German hands. As a result of this over-reaction he was at constant loggerheads with Goering's adjutant Von Schell who demanded three of the little cars to exhibit in Germany. Eventually, in seeking to persuade Boulanger that Germany's interest was more curious than malign, a Volkswagen was delivered to the factory at Javel; however even this token of good faith failed to move

Above: Front and rear views of the Rochetaillée prototype. The car was one of those which spent the war with a crude truck body at the Michelin plant at Clermont-Ferrand. In 1946 it was part of a load of scrap metal bought by M. Henri Malatre. As it was engineless Malatre had to find another example before he could run it, the chassis of which has since disappeared into a private collection somewhere. The car is now on permanent display at the motor museum at Rochelaillée-sur-Loane whilst another, complete with Salon style bodywork, surfaced in 1980 at the museum in Chatelleraut. (left: Bob MacQueen, right: National Motor Museum)

[1] Although at this distance this may seem a somewhat drastic reaction on the part of Boulanger one has only to bear in mind the chronic shortage of aircraft which beset France at this time. It is quite possible that just as in England where Lord Beaverbrook commandeered the national saucepans, the magnesium and duralumox were desperately needed by the plane makers. That more than the claimed number of prototypes survived, (Ferey claims four, the factory two), is amply demonstrated by the discovery in 1942 of an example which had been abandoned by a refugee from the factory at a small Citroën agency near Orléans, by Georges Toutblan, who was then reconducting the survey convened in '36 by Duclos. A further interesting avenue for exploration is the possibility, suggested by Viasnoff and Borgé, that two hundred semi complete prototypes of the *Salon* type were built into a wall at the Levallois plant.

Boulanger who steadfastly refused to release his precious charge to the Axis.[2]

By 1942 the German interest had waned, the factory at Javel was pressed into building rucks, and Boulanger deemed it prudent to resume development of the car ready for the cessation of hostilities. Towards this end Cadiou was instructed to redesign the car for production in steel, whilst Walter Becchia was recruited from Talbot to further develop the engine.

Working in secret, Becchia evolved an aircooled flat twin engine based largely upon the cylinder dimensions and valve gear of the water cooled unit of the *Salon* cars. Legend has it that he took only six days to effect this major transformation working mainly at night with his old friend and colleague from Talbot, Lucien Girard. Not only did the new engine overcome the problems of susceptibility to extreme cold which had beset the water cooled engine but with Girard's rationalisation to a single carburettor layout both the power output and the fuel consumption were improved.

For his part Jean Cadiou, working closely with the original team, managed to evolve in steel, the final and definitive floor plan which was to see the car into full production after the war. The TPV was now truly becoming the 2CV.

---

[2] Rumours persist that not only did the Germans capture at least one of the 1939 prototypes, which is quite likely as they soon occupied what was left of the Levallois factory with its TPV production line, but that it actually found its way to Wolfsburg where Dr Porsche was reported to be unimpressed. This hypothesis gives some credence to the apochryphal story of the German reaction to the car as "more a soapbox jalopy than a people's car" quoted by Borgé and Viasnoff.

3 The Debutante

The task facing Boulanger as the war ended seems unbelievably daunting, even viewed from the comfort of hindsight. The once efficient factories which had been the pride of André Citroën and an object lesson to all other motor manufacturers lay in ruins, the departing Germans and the RAF having completed the destruction begun by the Luftwaffe in 1940. Key personnel were drifting back from obligatory service in the factories of the Third Reich and such staples as steel or rubber were in incredibly short supply with the little available going first to the war effort in the far east or to firms like Renault who had access to both Marshall Aid and the ear of the Government.

The few cars Citroën managed to produce were almost totally constructed by hand but even so found a ready market among the few who will always thrive in such economic conditions. The first significant steps towards recovery however were being falteringly taken, the 'H' van making its reappearance in 1947 and commercial vehicle production quickly returning to almost its pre-war level. By the beginning of 1948 production of the *Traction* had surpassed pre-war numbers. All these cars were, however, reserved for export and priority users with government permits. In 1945 only 24 permits were issued!

Just how galling it must have been for Boulanger to bide his time while Renault, with the aid of Ferdinand Porsche, rushed the VW inspired 4CV into production in 1947 can only be imagined. Steel prototypes had been in existence since 1944 with peculiar variations upon the early bodywork. The manpower and factory capacity was available to produce the new car; only shortage of raw materials and cash held back the introduction of a car ideally suited to the enforced conditions of austerity then prevailing.

By the start of 1948 the final decisions had been reached on the bodywork, the hammock seats had been replaced by the tubular steel structures which remain to this day in slightly altered detail and the car was proving not only

Opposite: Evocative shot of the car on its Paris debut. (Fabien Sabates)

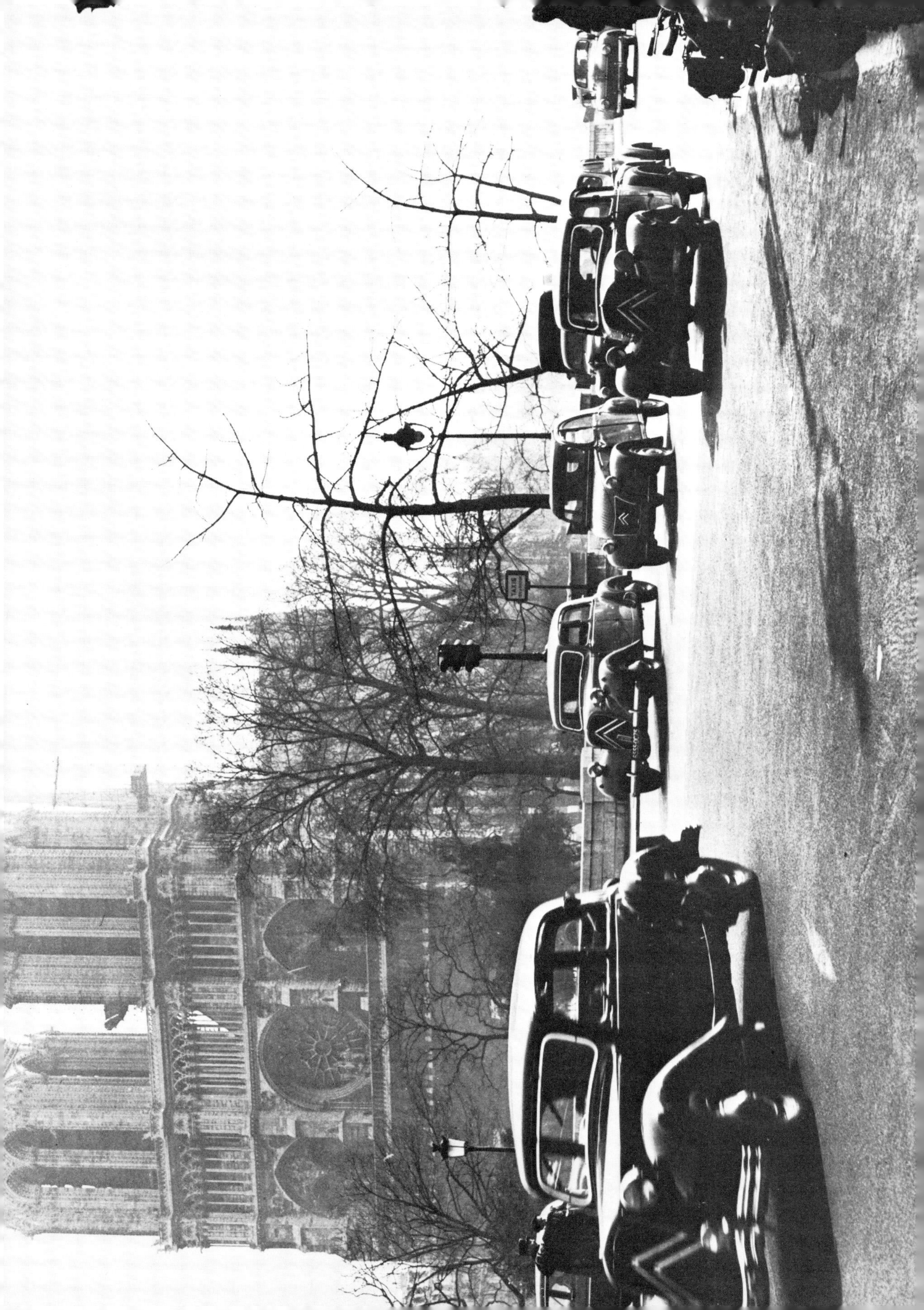

supremely reliable but also capable of matching all the idealistic demands made of it. By the simple expedient of mounting a step ladder upon the roof of his 11CV a photographer from *La Presse* had managed to catch a few glimpses (and later some rather murky photographs) and public curiosity was stirring.

The prime speculation in the press, probably fuelled by ex-Citroën employees who did not have access to any detailed overall information, was that the car being tested so secretly was a 3CV. Charles Faroux as usual knew better. To what extent this constant leakage of details to the press influenced Boulanger in his decision to exhibit at the 1948 *Salon* is unknown but it was undoubtedly a major contributory factor. In fact Boulanger was obviously considering the October unveiling in January when he ordered photographs to be taken ready for a brochure and supervised them himself.

The reactions of both public and press were quickly to follow the dramatic unveiling. "Do you supply the can opener with it?" asked one American journalist whilst another complimented Citroën on producing the ugliest car in the world. *Autocar* contented itself with the dry remark that "The designer has kissed the lash of austerity with almost masochistic fervour", before going on to extol the revolutionary engineering of the little car. Almost all the contemporary press reports dwell on the small engine yet at its introductory price of 185,000 francs it was obviously the cheapest practical form of transport capable of taking four passengers, on display.

Below: Beautiful early publicity shot taken in January 1948 and suffering a little from some overzealous attention from the scalpel and airbrush. Note the chevron pattern of the bars and the grille, the three stud wheels, tubular framed front bench seat, mechanically driven windscreen wipers (powered from the speedo drive) and early pattern front roof fixing. (Citroën)

Above: Overhead shot again from early 1948 clearly showing the first pattern door handles, canvas boot cover, offset rear lights, primitive window catches and the weld seams at the curvature of the bonnet which characterised these early examples. *(Citroën)*

Left: Summer 1948. With doors and roof removed, standing in its designated environment, though the lady in the pearls fails to convince in the role of peasant, the car demonstrates its genuine four adult capacity for the forthcoming brochures. *(Citroën)*

Left: Again, January 1948. Le patron himself joins three of his employees for the benefit of the photographer. Even the heavily retouched background and more careful scalpel work cannot quite convince the viewer that this is anything but a 'drop in'. (Citroën)

Below: 1952. Although the four-gonnette (bottom right) is the latest debutante the focus of the stand is still the 2CV as the Paris Salon gets under way. (Citroën)

Above: The first publicity shot of the fourgonnette taken in 1951 showing the old style lozenge shaped rear windows. (Citroën)

One by one the dealers and the press voiced their objections. Citroën were ready for them. To those who scoffed at its low maximum speed it was pointed out that very few provincial peasants had any desire to travel from Paris to Marseilles in a day. The slab sided coachwork became more acceptable once the ease of repair and cheapness of its components were realised. Even the uniform metallic grey finish had its practical side in that it was easily touched in when scratched and such artifacts as wings, doors or bonnet lids could, if necessary, be painted before attachment.

This catalogue of practicalities still didn't stop the catalogue of insults, the best of which must be the 'bathing machine' which one Citroën agent likened it to, but it did sell out the following year's production. So successful was the launch that by the time of the car's introduction the following year, after an extensive tour of the dealers and some highly publicised mountain climbing in the Alps, the production had to be strictly rationed. Highest priority was given to country doctors, then vets and midwives, horticulturists and so on. The result of this clever strategy was that by the end of 1950 good second hand examples were fetching higher prices than new ones and the dealers were quoting a two and a half year delivery whilst production was nudging three hundred vehicles per week.[1] In fact this state of affairs persisted right through to 1954 when *Autocar* observed "This small Citroën is the only car on the French market for which quick deliveries cannot be guaranteed, and which is selling for more, after a year's wear than when new".[2]

By 1949, when the model first came on to the market, the price had risen to 228,000 francs yet this was still amost fifty thousand francs cheaper than the Renault 4. Thirteen years after Duclos had begun his survey of the market Boulanger had provided the French with the car of the future.

The car which eventually went on sale in 1949 was, however, subtly different in certain respects to that which titillated the public's interest at the 1948 *Salon*. Jean Muratet and Marcel Chinon's overall chassis and suspension layout was retained. So too were the friction dampers evolved by Leon Renault and described as 'batteurs' to overcome Boulanger's dislike for shock absorbers. The engine was as designed by Becchia with a few minor alterations to 'productionise' it, mated to Forceau's original gearbox which, due to Becchia's influence, had now gained a fourth gear (this again being described as an overdrive to get around Boulanger's firm directive that the box was only to have three forward ratios).

Such changes as there were concerned mainly Bertoni's[3] bodywork. the side lights on the front wings disappeared. The rear wings were rounded outwards and the bottoms made horizontal rather than using the gentle scallop of the '48 cars. The door handles were changed along with the rather cumbersome device which originally sealed the roof. A more efficient bonnet catch was incorporated while at the front the herringbone pattern of the air intake was replaced by horizontal bars. The bottom rear corners of the front windows were rounded off to give a more pleasing effect and the upholstery was standardised to a slate grey.

This then was the car which was to conquer post-war Europe alongside the ubiquitous VW.

[1] The production figures were 1949 - 924. 1950 - 6,196. 1952 - 21, 124.
[2] *Autocar* 1-10-54.
[3] In fairness it should be noted that the final decisions upon the bodywork were taken by Maurice Steck whom Boulanger appointed after rejecting Bertoni's 'cyclops' treatment of the bonnet. Ironically the first newspaper pictures were from Ferté-Vidame Salon. The caption spoke of a 3CV.

The first full British road test of the 2CV was carried in Motor. We reproduce it here by kind permission of the present editor.

The Motor Road Test No. 14/53

Make: Citroen **Type:** 2 c.v.

Makers: Citroen Cars Ltd., Trading Estate, Slough, Bucks

Dimensions and Seating

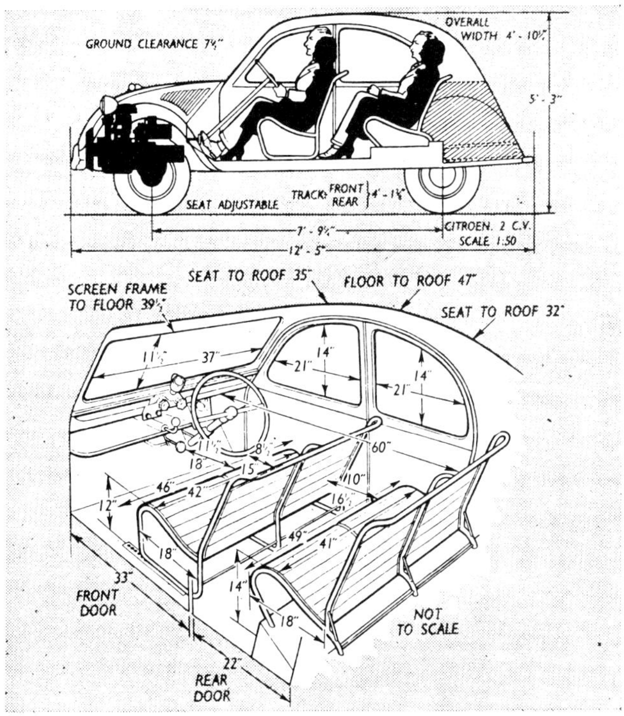
GROUND CLEARANCE 7½"
OVERALL WIDTH 4'-10½"
5'-3"
SEAT ADJUSTABLE
TRACK: FRONT REAR 4'-1⅛"
7'-9½"
12'-5"
CITROEN. 2 C.V. SCALE 1:50
SEAT TO ROOF 35"
FLOOR TO ROOF 47"
SCREEN FRAME TO FLOOR 39½"
SEAT TO ROOF 32"
37"
21"
14"
60"
46"
42"
18"
15"
12"
10"
49"
41"
33"
FRONT DOOR
REAR DOOR
22"
NOT TO SCALE

Test Conditions

Cool, dry weather with little wind. Smooth Tarmac surface. Intermediate-grade pump fuel.

Test Data

ACCELERATION TIMES on Two Upper Ratios

	Top	3rd
10-30 m.p.h.	28.9 sec.	19.4 sec.
20-40 m.p.h.	56.8 sec.	32.9 sec.

ACCELERATION TIMES Through Gears

0-30 m.p.h.	19.6 sec.
0-40 m.p.h.	42.4 sec.
Standing quarter mile	34.4 sec.

MAXIMUM SPEEDS

Flying Quarter Mile

Mean of four opposite runs	40.9 m.p.h.
Best time equals	42.3 m.p.h.

FUEL CONSUMPTION

76.0 m.p.g. at constant 20 m.p.h.
75.0 m.p.g. at constant 30 m.p.h.
70.0 m.p.g at constant 35 m.p.h.

Overall consumption for 1,328 miles, driving hard, 24.25 gallons, = 54.7 m.p.g.

Speed in Gears

Max. speed in 3rd gear approx.	41 m.p.h.
Max. speed in 2nd gear	22 m.p.h.
Max. speed in 1st gear	10 m.p.h.

INSTRUMENTS

Speedometer at 30 m.p.h.	1% fast
Speedometer at 40 m.p.h.	4% slow
Distance recorder	2½% fast

WEIGHT

Unladen kerb weight	10 cwt.
Front/rear weight distribution	59/41
Weight laden as tested	13½ cwt.

HILL CLIMBING (At steady speeds)

Max. 3rd gear speed on 1 in 20	28 m.p.h.
Max. gradient on top gear	1 in 21.5 (Tapley 105 lb./ton)
Max. gradient on 3rd gear	1 in 15.5 (Tapley 145 lb./ton)
Max. gradient on 2nd gear	1 in 9.5 (Tapley 235 lb./ton)

BRAKES at 30 m.p.h.

0.99 g retardation (= 30½ ft. stopping distance) with 75 lb. pedal pressure
0.63 g retardation (= 48 ft. stopping distance) with 50 lb. pedal pressure
0.21 g retardation (=143 ft. stopping distance) with 25 lb. pedal pressure

In Brief

Price £398 plus purchase tax £166 19s. 2d. equals	£564 19s. 2d.
Capacity	375 c.c.
Unladen kerb weight	10 cwt.
Fuel consumption	54.7 m.p.g.
Maximum speed	40.9 m.p.h.
Max. speed on 1 in 20 gradient	28 m.p.h.
Maximum top gear gradient	1 in 21.5
Acceleration :	
10-30 m.p.h. in top	28.9 sec.
0-40 m.p.h. through gears	42.4 sec.

Gearing 11.9 m.p.h. in top at 1,000 r.p.m., 73 m.p.h. at 2,500 ft. per min. piston speed.

Specification

Engine

Cylinders	2 (air cooled)
Bore	62 mm.
Stroke	62 mm.
Cubic capacity	375 c.c.
Piston Area	9.36 sq. in.
Valves	Pushrod o.h.v.
Compression ratio	6.2 /1
Max. power	9 b.h.p.
at	3,500 r.p.m.
Piston speed at max. b.h.p.	1,425 ft. per min
Carburetter	Solex downdraught
Ignition	6-volt coil
Sparking plugs	14 mm. K.L.G. FA50
Fuel Pump	mechanical
Oil filter	gauze on pump

Transmission

Clutch	Single dry plate
Top gear (s/m)	5.72
3rd gear (s/m)	7.50
2nd gear (s/m)	12.55
1st gear (s/m)	25.9
Propeller shaft	nil (front-wheel drive)
Final drive	Spiral bevel

Chassis

Brakes	Lockheed hydraulic (front brakes on differential assembly)
Brake drum diameter	7½ in
Friction lining area	60.9 sq. in.
Suspension	All wheels independently sprung, by leading arms at front and trailing arms at rear. Central coil springs coupled to both front and rear wheels.
Shock absorbers	Oil-damped units on each wheel to check patter.
Tyres	Michelin, 125 x 400

Steering

Steering gear	rack and pinion
Turning circle	33 feet
Turns of steering wheel, lock to lock.	2½

Performance factors (at laden weight as tested)

Piston area, sq. in per ton	13.9
Brake lining area, sq. in. per ton	90.2
Specific displacement, litres per ton mile	1,400

Maintenance

Fuel tank : 4½ gallons. **Sump :** 3½ pints, S.A.E. 20 **Gearbox and differential :** 1¾ pints, E.P.80. **Rear axle :** Retinax A or similar. **Steering gear :** Retinax A or similar. **Chassis lubrication:** By grease gun every 1,000 miles to 4 points. Pedal gear, suspension spring links by oil caps. **Ignition timing :** 8° B.T.D.C. **Spark plug gap :** .025-.028. **Contact breaker gap :** .015 + .002. **Valve timing:** I.O. 3° B.T.D.C.; I.C. 45° A.B.D.C.; E.O. 45° B.B.D.C.; E.C. 11° A.T.D.C. **Tappet clearances :** (Hot) : Inlet .006 in. Exhaust .008 in. **Front wheel toe-out:** 11/64 in. **Camber angle:** 1° 30'. **Castor angle :** 0° 15'. **Tyre pressures :** Front 14 lb., Rear 15½ lb. **Brake fluid :** Lockheed. **Battery :** 6-volt 57 amp/hr. **Lamp bulbs :** Head lamp, 36w. double-filament (side 6w.). Rear number plate, 3w. Tail lamp, 3w. Stop, 3w.

Ref. B-F/4/53.

September 27, 1950.

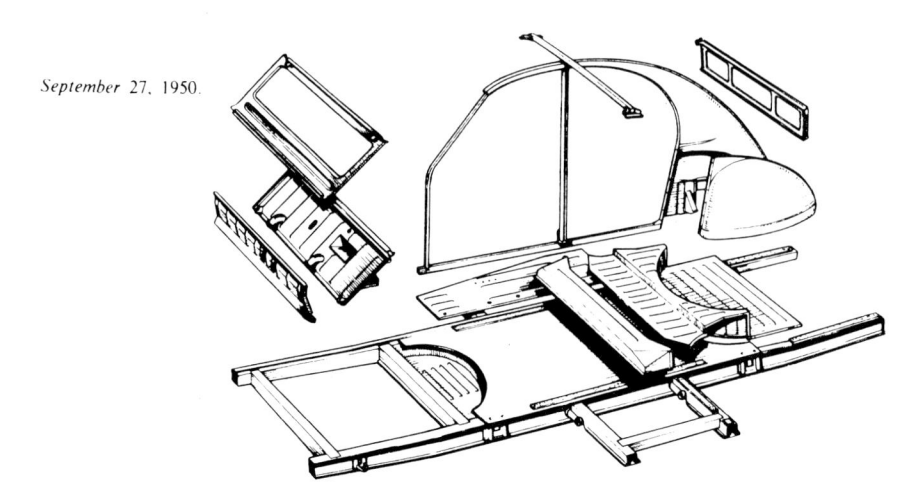

Drawings immediately above and left show the extreme simplicity of the Citroen chassis-cum-body construction coupled with the folding canvas top which makes the car openable at will and provides access to the large luggage locker. The detail sketch shows the box section chassis members and their relation to the floor and the built-up pressings which stiffen the fore part of the car.

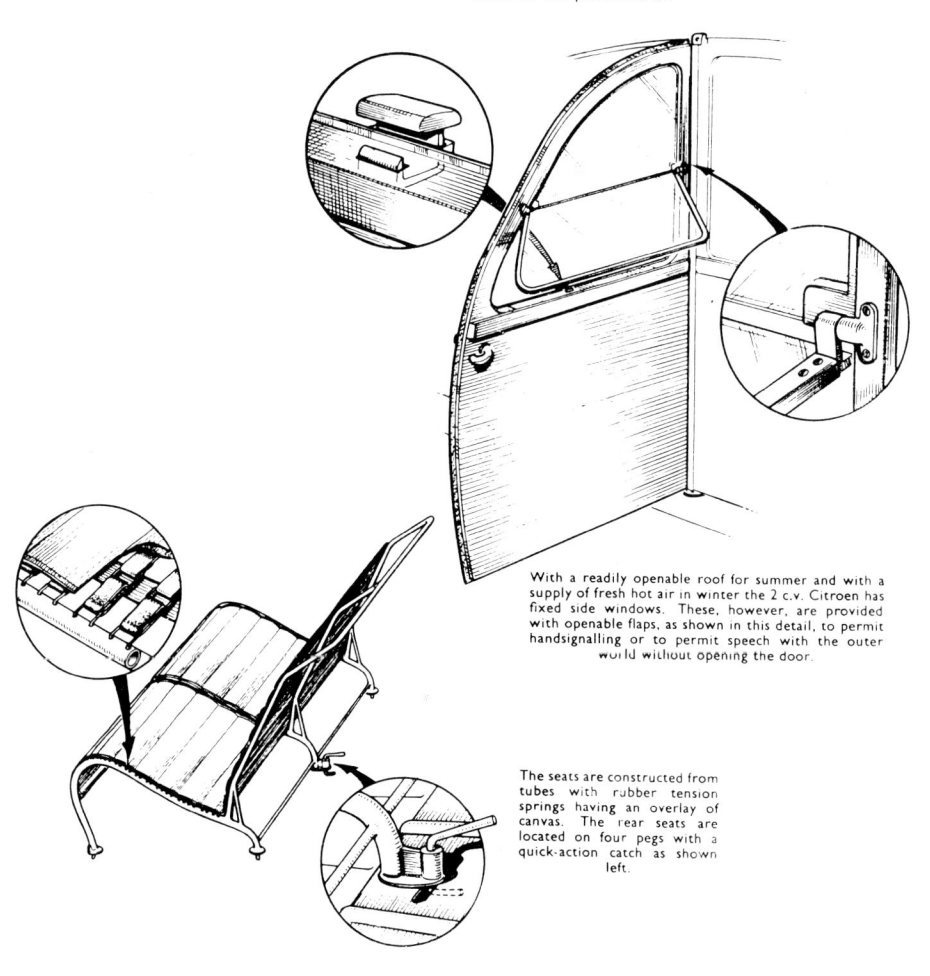

With a readily openable roof for summer and with a supply of fresh hot air in winter the 2 c.v. Citroen has fixed side windows. These, however, are provided with openable flaps, as shown in this detail, to permit handsignalling or to permit speech with the outer world without opening the door.

The seats are constructed from tubes with rubber tension springs having an overlay of canvas. The rear seats are located on four pegs with a quick-action catch as shown left.

The Motor

The only instruments provided are an ammeter and speedometer, and the drive to the latter can be coupled to the windscreen wiper arms as shown in the drawing below.

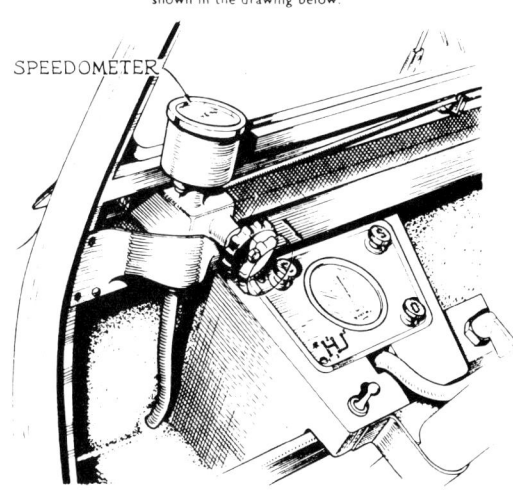

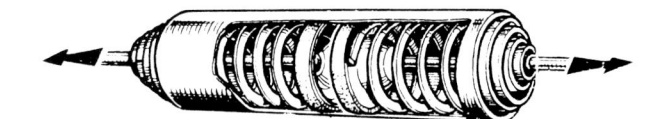

SPEEDOMETER

The most novel technical feature of the car is the suspension system. Tension rods connect the individual wheel arms to a coil spring which is compressed when the wheel moves upwards in relation to the car. Pairs of springs connecting to the front and rear wheels on each side of the vehicle are contained in a cylinder which is mounted on the frame through the volute springs shown and the cylinder as a whole therefore moves in response to any out-of-balance between front and rear wheel motion.

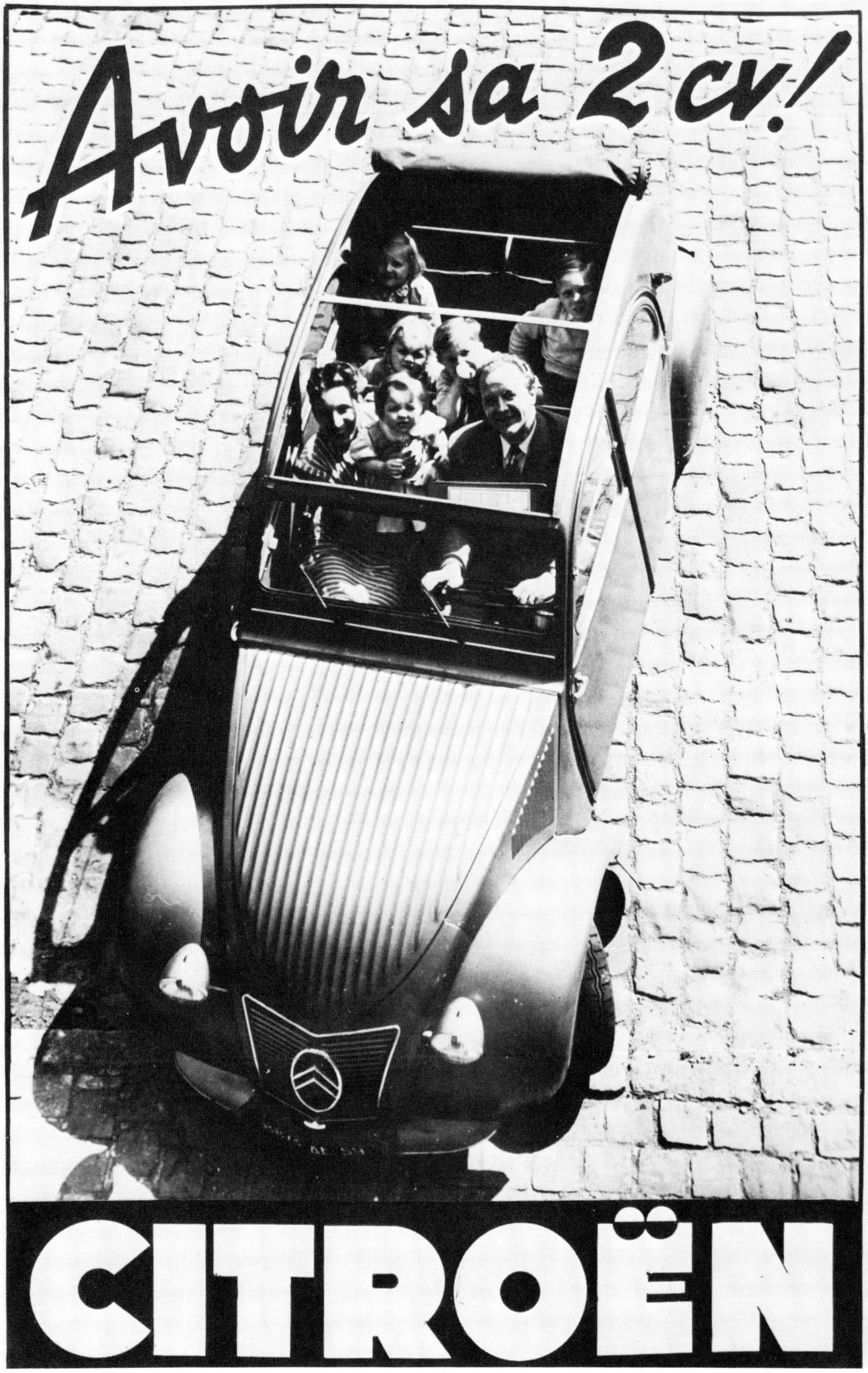
Avoir sa 2 cv!
CITROËN

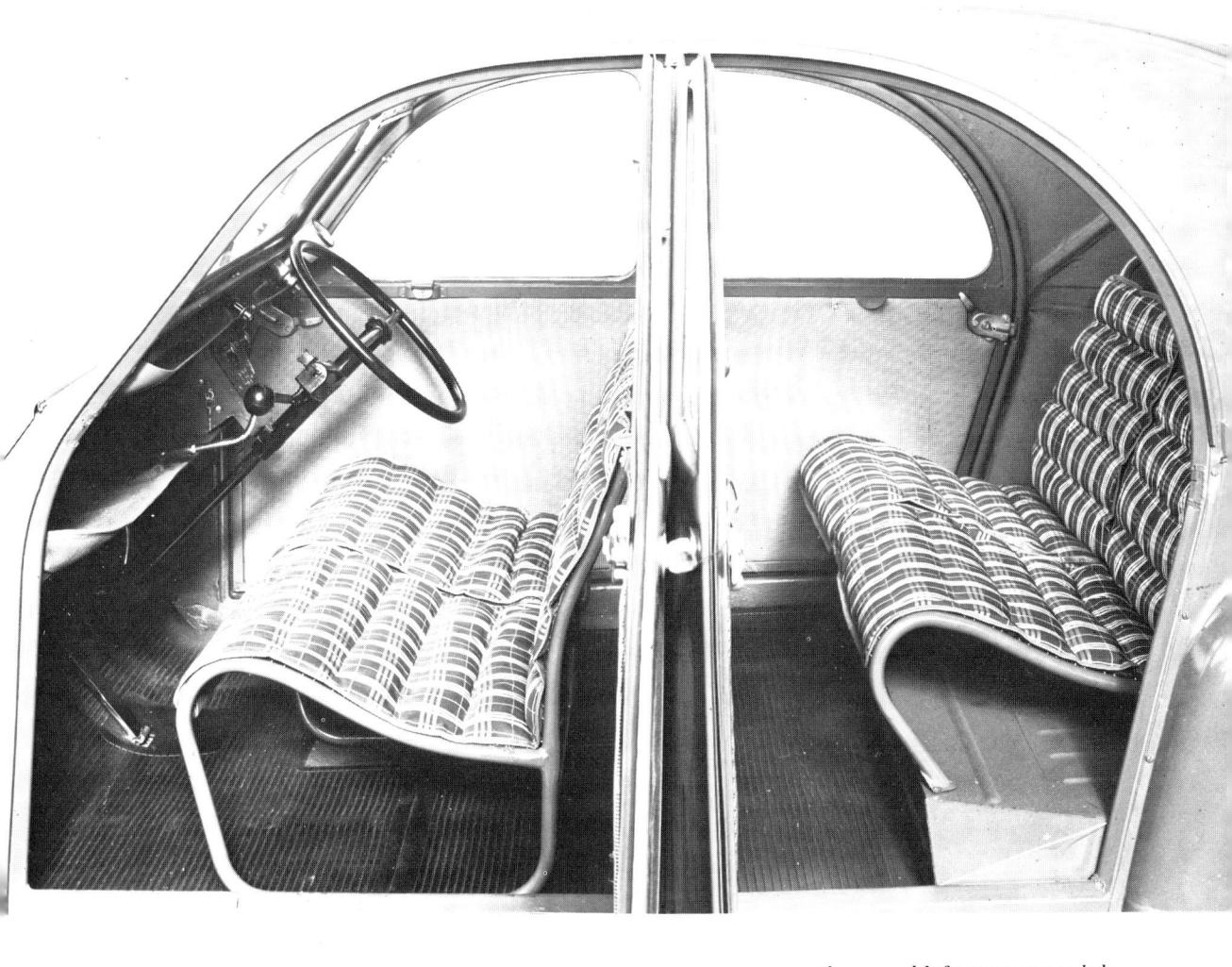

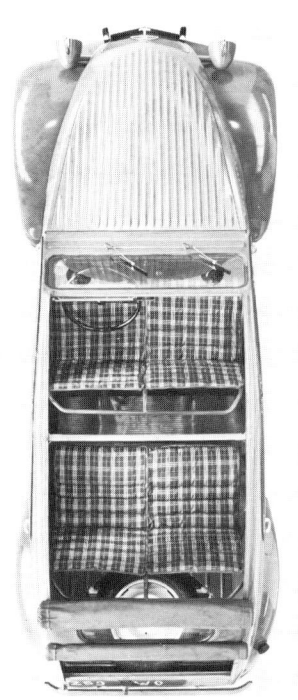

Above and left: 1954 saw subtle evolutionary changes. Following the introduction of an ignition key and locks in 1951, the sensation of tartan upholstery and textured door linings were added to confound such ill informed critics who continued to bleat about austerity. Flashing indicators were also introduced. (Citroën)

Opposite: With the car successfully selling itself the publicity department did not really have to try too hard. This 1951 advert was accompanied by a letter purporting to come from the father of the happy family pictured here warmly commending the 2CV to other large families! (Citroën)

(a)

Above and opposite: On the technical front the 425cc 12 bhp engine was introduced on the AZ model (a) whilst the gearbox was modified to take the new centrifugal clutch making the use of the clutch pedal unnecessary at low revs in first and second gears (b). In an attempt to stop the pitching motion of the very early models an experimental open and forward biased system of side springing was installed from January to April 1955 (c). Other modification included the addition of a second rear brake light the abolition of the oval surround for the double chevron motive on the radiator grille, lighting for the speedometer and a light for the rear number plate of the AZU van (see appendix 1). (Citroën)

(c)

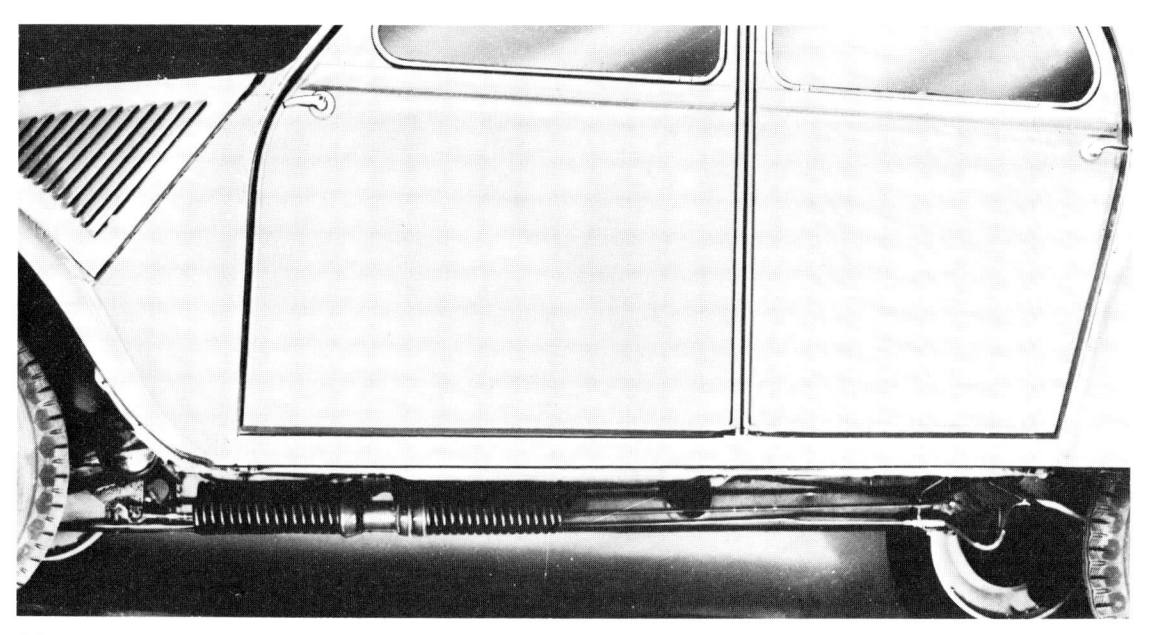

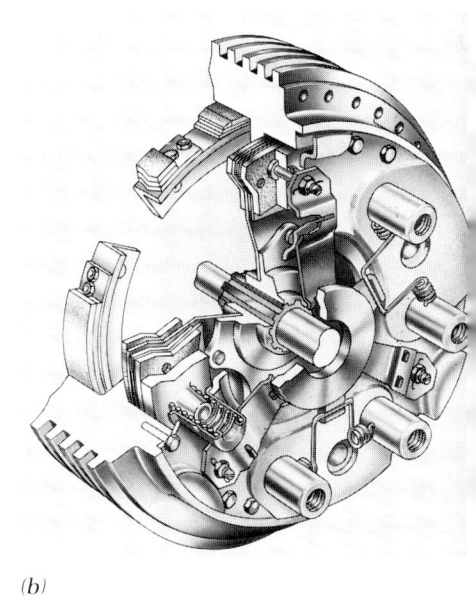

(b)

Above: As civilisation continued to encroach upon the 2CV it acquired a demister as shown in this 1956 shot of an AZ engine. (Citroën)

Above: 1957 AZ showing trafficators, forward facing front door handles, twin rear stop lights with central number plate light and the newly introduced larger rear window. (Citroën)

Left: The 1958 AZ with centralised number plate and steel boot lid. (Citroën)

41

4 The First Adventurers

The adventures started with Michel Bernier and Jacques Huguier when an impulse to travel sent them on a marathon tour around the Mediterranean. In fact the idea started before that when Bernier as a young car salesman with a slipped disc consulted Dr Huguier and confessed a desire to spend his holidays travelling in some exotic land in his car. By the summer of 1952 the route was planned, the travel documents, maps and special equipment were ready and the car was loaded. In thirty seven days the pair put 13,588 kilometers on the clock and visited every country bordering the Mediterranean. They dealt with hostile customs officials, appalling roads and, in Egypt, a revolution. At the end of the voyage they delivered the car to the factory at Javel for Citroën to examine the state of its components, then they walked home penniless leaving the management at Javel to ponder the publicity value of the feat....

The next long journey was a crossing of the Sahara. The man who made it was one Louis Audouin-Dubreuil, who had been on the *Croisière Noire* in 1925 and '26 and, before that, had been in the original Sahara expedition despatched by André Citroën in 1922. Unlike Bernier and Huguier he had some help from Citroën. In crossing from Tunis to Mimimoum he travelled some 6,000 kilometers over some of the world's most inhospitable terrain.

A Captain Tschiffely had ridden two horses the length of the American continent documenting his feat in a book called *Tschiffely's Ride*. Enter Jacques Cornet and Henri Lochon who took two mechanical horses on the same route claiming en route a new record for altitude in an air cooled car. The result was a book, *2 hommes, 2CV, 2 continents*, the first of many. The journey took almost exactly a year from May '53 to May '54.

If a man was to drive a 2CV from Capetown to Algeria and then enter that same 2CV in the Monte Carlo Rally starting from Oslo, would that be enough to draw some outside sponsorship? So ran Michel Bernier's reasoning when he

Opposite: It could almost be Daytona Beach but in reality Seguela and Baudot are making camp in the centre of the Sahara. (Citroën)

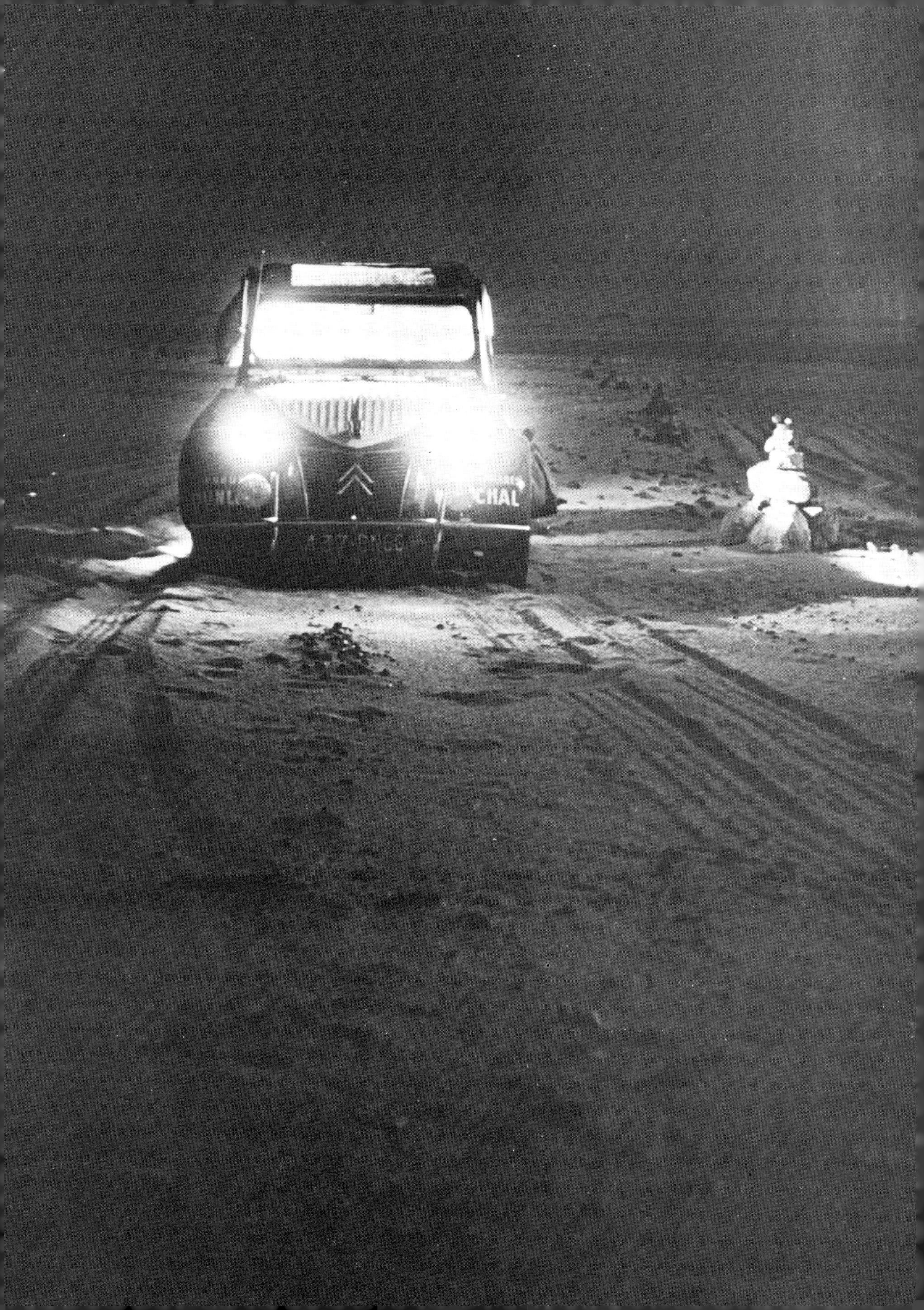
CHAL

commenced his next exploit. With backing from Mobil and some factory assistance with the preparation, remembering this time to pack a camera, Bernier undertook this feat in December 1953 with Jacques Duvey for company. This time the two received a hero's welcome as they entered the Porte d'Italie and only a broken dynamo stopped them taking class honours on the Monte.

Whilst Cornet was negotiating mountains in Southern America and Bernier was heading north from the Cape, an expedition of three *fourgonnettes* led by Guy Viau was heading south from Egypt to the Cape. They took slightly longer than Bernier arriving in May after 40,000 gruelling kilometers.

Africa and America having become *passé*, an unnamed Citroën salesman spent his annual holiday traversing Australia from north to south with an outward bound trip from Alice Springs to Port Darwin. The two week trip took him 5,485 miles at an average consumption of 4.7 litres to 100Ks (Approx 56mpg).

In France the cost of the 2CV per kilometer worked out at approximately 0.5Fr against the cost per kilometer of the SNCF (French Railways) of 3.00Fr. This reasoning lay uppermost in the mind of Robert Godet when he took his car from Paris to Tibet in March 1954. His co-driver was one Marguerite Batigne the first lady to endure one of the long voyages.

The list is endless, even in the first few years of the car's life. The name of Jacques Cornet crops up time and time again; *2 hommes, 2CV en Asie*, deals with a journey from Paris to Tokyo. Further travels in the Argentine, Egypt and Afghanistan all produced books. Godet for his part duly recorded his adventures on the Indian sub-continent. Realising the value of exploits such as these Citroën began awarding a cash prize for the most imaginative 2CV exploit in any given year. Inaugurated in 1957 the prize of 10,000Fr was awarded until 1971 when the money was deemed better spent in organising the famous raids. The last winner was a young man named Christian Gallisian who managed a 110,000 kilometer trip around the world in a *fourgonnette* which had been bought second hand for 300Fr with 250,000 kilometers already on the clock.

Perhaps the most celebrated of the prize winners were 1959 recipients Jacques Seguela and Jean-Claude Baudot who made the first ever round the world trip by a French car. The book duly produced *La Terre En Rond*, is still in print, a salient reminder of the fifties when the world was still a relatively safe place for the international traveller.

Left and below: Seguela and Baudot in Burma. *(Citroën)*

Above: 1966 prix Citroën winner Philippe Genty with his expedition leader 'Alexandre' pausing to view the Hoggar mountains. (Citroën)

Left: Michel Bernier and Jacques Duvey on the Monte in January 1954. In 1955 Bernier had the satisfaction of finishing 271st out of 652 starters in the Mille Miglia with a standard production 2CV fitted with a larger carburettor. (National Motor Museum)

Left: Marie-Thérèse Hoby and Antoinette Ruesein's Expedition Architectural enjoying a primitive ferry in the Indian Ocean... (Citroën)

Below: ... and passing the time of day with an Indian Elephant. (Citroën)

Left and below: The ancient Mayan monuments like this one at Tikal plus the highways and byways of Peru might be highly scenic but the bridges are appalling if the one below is a representative sample.

Above and left: Could this be the redoubtable Christian Gallisian on his bargain price global expedition or is it that man Gornet again? Such evidence as the writers can glean suggest that it is the former.

49

One British adventurer who perhaps has had less than his fair share of exposure was Dr Murray Last sometime Professor of History at Ahmadu Bello University in Nigeria. In 1965, realising that the production run was ending, Dr Last ordered a *Sahara*. The car was duly completed in 1966 and he took delivery in Zaria. Having used a standard 2CV in that country prior to this it seemed a natural progression to have the twin next.

With the 1967 coup in Nigeria a certain homesickness for the more temperate political clime of Britain beset him causing him to load the car with thirty gallons of petrol in plastic drums and point the nose northwards. With the exception of the civil war the journey as far as Southern Algeria caused few difficulties with the necessity of cleaning the air filters twice a day the main chore. However, the stage of the journey through the Hoggar mountains posed a problem for, between Agedes and Tamanrasset, a distance of some seven hundred miles, there was little chance of finding any petrol and precious little hope of rescue should the car break down.

Undaunted the good doctor pressed on. Running over roads which were little more than tracks of deep dust marked by occasional piles of stone or indistinct landmarks meant that both engines had to be used at all times. This coupled with the heavy load of water and fuel dropped fuel consumption to only about twenty five miles per gallon. Tamanrasset was reached with just a gallon to spare.

The mountainous country about Tamanrasset was the next hurdle and here the low first gear really came into its own as a breakline fractured, shedding all the car's fluid. From three in the afternoon until one in the morning the car was driven without brakes until a roadside French Army depot was reached where the brake pipe was brazed and the fluid replaced. Perhaps after this the doctor deserved a more placid return and it would appear that, with the exception of the British customs officials at Folkestone, he achieved it.

As if one journey wasn't enough, Dr Last added a new meaning to the word commuting when he retraced the journey in 1969 from Britain to Nigeria. This time there was no war to distract him and, with the exception of a two day sand storm which caused him to make several involuntary detours in the Sahara, the passage was completed with no untoward incidents.

After a long and distinguished career in Nigeria the car returned finally to England in 1980, this time in the cargo hold of a jet, where it is now in the possession of Bob MacQueen.

Above: Scenes from Dr Last's epic Saharan treks. (Dr Murray Last)

THE RAIDS

André Citroën captured the imagination of the world with his 'Raids'. A whole generation followed the headlines of the day to check the progress of 1923's *Croisière Noire* crossing of Africa and the *Croisière Jaune* which terminated in 1932 in Pekin. True to the old Hollywood maxim of 'what will work once will work twice' Jacques Wolgensinger resurrected the spirit of these adventures in the early seventies with his own version starring the 2CV.

The first of these epics was the Paris-Kabul of 1970 sponsored jointly by Citroën and Total. The rules of entry were quite simple, one must be a 2CV owner of not more than thirty and not less than eighteen years of age. Times were set for each stage of the journey and a prize of ten 2CV6s was offered for the best performance and journal on the journey with a bonus of 5,000Fr to the winner, 3,000Fr to the runner up and so on.

Hardly surprisingly the original entry was over 5,000. By a process of natural wastage this finally shrank to some 1,300 of which some 494 crews were chosen to start the arduous course. Although one crew failed to return in tragic circumstances the raid was an enormous success and such was the enthusiasm generated that another went into the planning stage immediately.

(Citroën)

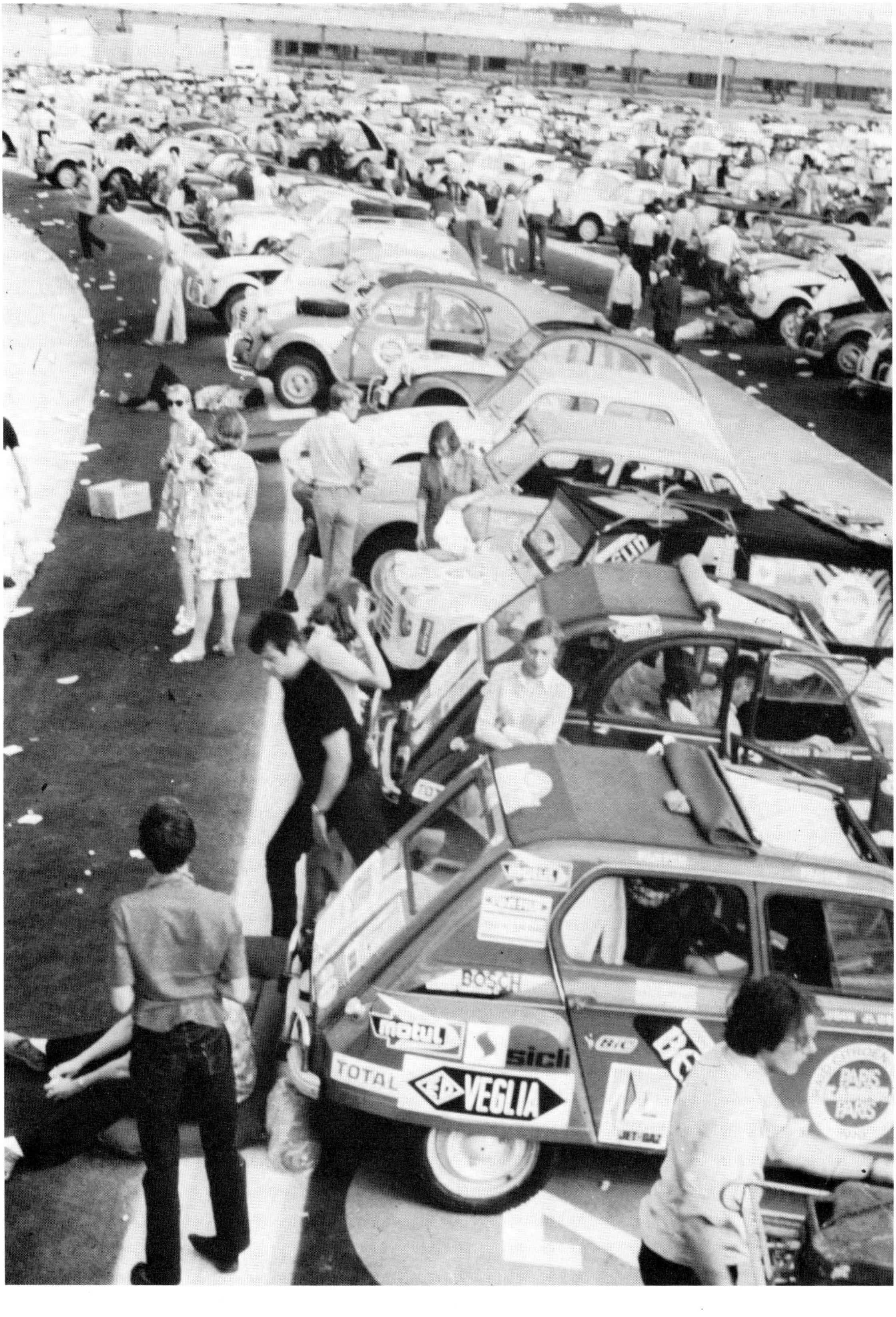
BOSCH
motul
sicli
TOTAL
VEGLIA
PARIS
PARIS
JET-GAZ

The Paris-Persepolis raid of 1971 drew further sponsorship from the radio station RTL and Iran house and was timed to coincide with the Shah's celebration of two thousand years of his dynasty. This time some 3,800 crews applied to join up and again the entry was whittled down to just 467 crews. This time the media made sure that the raid was an even larger success than the first. There were no fatalities and 410 vehicles returned in the time alloted as opposed to the 320 of the previous year. Another even more ambitious project was obviously called for.

Using 1972 as a sabbatical year in which to map out the route 1973 proved to be Wolgensinger's biggest triumph, the *Raid Afrique*. This time only the cream of adventurous French youth was enlisted and the examinations for places in the entry were stringent both in the natural aptitude of the applicants in their profession or trade and of their mechanical skills. The story of that raid is best told in the following pictures.

Opposite: The assembled starters for the Paris-Kabul. As can be noticed from the way they are parked some confusion still existed as to the direction of Afghanistan. (Citroën)

Below: A traditional Persian form of transport seen with the tradtional French equivalent. (Citroën)

53

Above: Persepolians pause by a medieval Turkish fortress. *(Citroën)*

Left: Dyane nearing Persepolis. *(Citroën)*

Above: The additional sponsorship of Berliet allowed each column of cars its own tender. Here the cars are formed up waiting for another day of Sahara conditions. *(Citroën)*

(Citroën)

55

Left: The car designed by committee meets the horse designed by one. (Citroën)

Above and left: In soft sand some manpower and a little co-operation kept the party going. (Citroën)

Left: Scenes such as this are a vital ingredient...

Below: ... to scenes such as this. *(Citroën)*

Above: The magnificence of a gathering desert storm. (Citroën)

Left: Looking like a set from Beau Geste, a ruined wadi. (Citroën)

*Left: Into darkest Africa...
(Citroën)*

Below: Latterday emissaries of France make contact with civilisation on the Ivory coast. (Citroën)

5 The Plastic 2CVs

As early as 1949 an incredibly ugly fibre glass coupé based on the running gear of the 2CV was exhibited at the 36th Paris *Salon* by a coachbuilder named Clauzet. The trend continues....

60

Above and left: Here a mark 2 is seen above the standard car upon which the shape of the special has been traced. (Maurice Leroy)

Opposite: Jean Dagonet built his first confection in 1952. Using aluminium cylinders stroked to give 425cc in cast iron jackets twin carburettors and twin exhausts in a lowered and lightened 2CV frame, he managed to produce a car which was both striking and efficient. A Mk1 off to do battle amongst the Jaguars, Mercedes and Ferraris in the 1955 Mille Miglia. (Maurice Leroy)

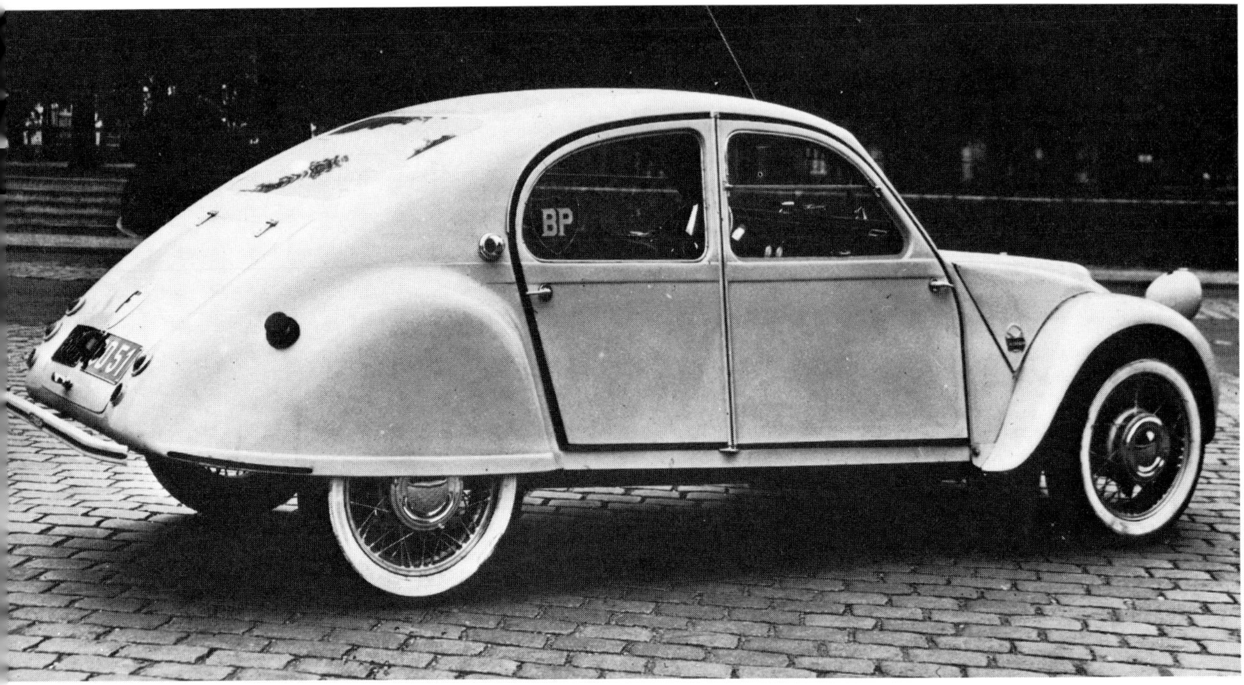
BP

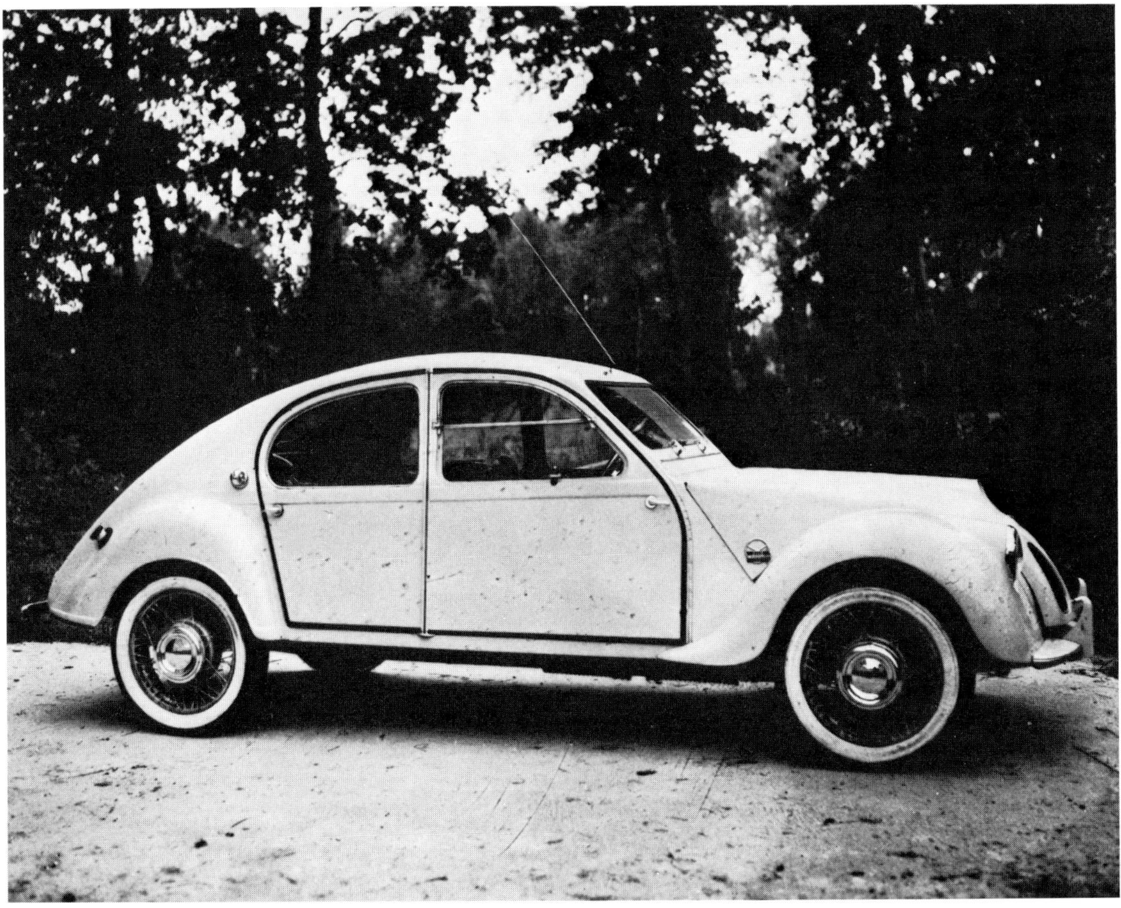

Opposite above: The second model from the Reims factory dispensed with the canvas roof and replaced the slotted wheels of the Mk1 with wires. Note the wood rimmed steering wheel, the neat direction indicators and subtly reshaped rear wheel arches. (Maurice Leroy)

Opposite below: The third model showing the faired in headlamps scalloped rear wings and Ferrari like grille. (Maurice Leroy)

Left: Front and rear views of the altogether less charming 1957 Dagonet. By this time the engine had been bored out to 500cc. (Maurice Leroy)

Over page: The Marquis de Pontac decided to leave his vines long enough to produce this striking machine with its three part modular coachwork and restricted travel suspension. It was sold in kit form from 1958 after several small capacity sports car racing successes. The road going car was credited with a top speed of 130 kph and the road holding was described by the motoring press as "sensational". The headlights were mounted on swivels and the doors opened downward to complete the futuristic package. A later model was shown at the Salon with floral paint finish complete with model in matching beach wear. (National Motor Museum)

63

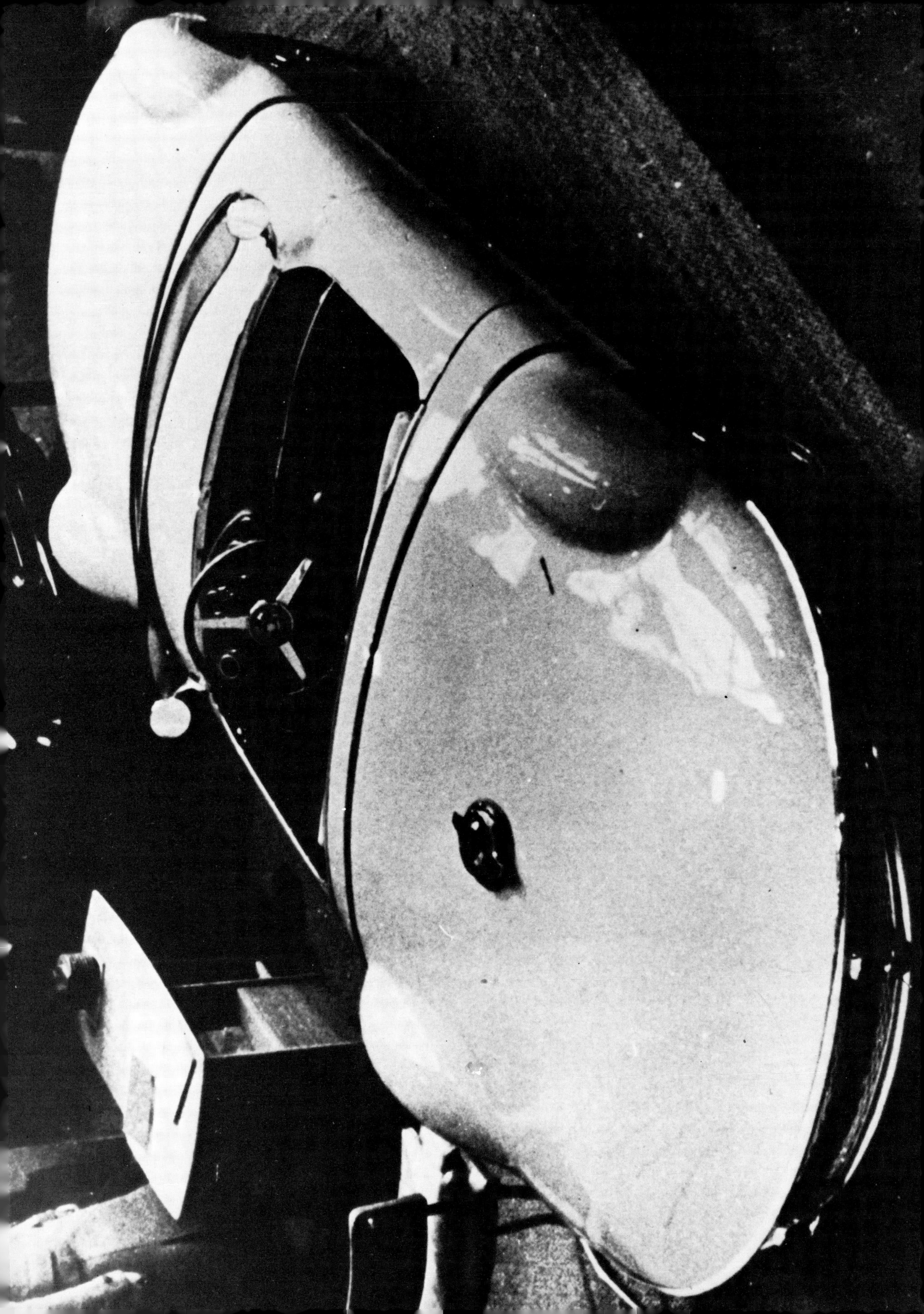

Above: The 1957 UMAP as shown at the Salon. (National Motor Museum)

Left: A Belgian exercise upon the theme by Daniel D'Leterer. (National Motor Museum)

Above: In a last ditch effort to sell the 2CV in Britain, Slough produced the Bijou. (Bob MacQueen)

Left: The dashboard of the Bijou. (Bob MacQueen)

Above: Neville Tricket of Siva (better known for their beach buggies and mock Model T kits) next to his pretty 2CV based vintage Renault inspired Crystic Car. (Fabien Sabates)

6 The Anglo Saxons & the 2CV

With the 2CV firmly established in its home market and successfully launched into production in Belgium in 1952 and with a long and lucrative presence in the British market with a subtly anglicised version of the Traction, the UK naturally seemed the next market for the little car. It came as no surprise therefore when a right hand drive version of the 2CV, assembled at Slough was announced for the 1953 Motor Show.

Taken at face value the car as it was introduced, with slightly improved trim and various colour options, should have found a ready niche in the market. Priced fairly highly at £564.19s.2d it was still competitive with such indigenous products as the Ford Anglia (£511) and the Morris Minor (£529.10s.10d), although mightily undercut by such vehicles as the Ford Popular (£390), the Standard Eight (£489.7s.6d), and the Austin A30 (£475.14s.2d) whilst the two stroke Lloyd offered similar performance and economy for a mere £310.

The motoring press, almost without exception, greeted the newcomer with road tests which ran little short of wide eyed rapture. "A vehicle with Almost Every Virtue Except Speed, Silence and Good Looks", headlined *Motor* who diplomatically pointed out that part of the reason for the car's production at Slough was to take advantage of Commonwealth Preference in the emergent third world.

Autocar spread its road test and technical description over two issues before running the car from Lands End to John O'Groats, the two gentlemen thus entrusted expressing themselves extremely satisfied adding that; "Comment other than praise is confined to criticism of the driving mirror view for an average height driver..." hardly a damning condemnation.

Not to be outdone that great doyen of British motoring scribes, William Boddy, took the car over the route used for the 1924 RAC Small Car Trials, covering some two thousand miles in eighteen days. His report ends with the words; "Certainly from now on I shall look with scorn at cars of low

Opposite: The newcomer from Slough justifies some of its expense by successfully competing in the London Rally 15 September 1955. (National Motor Museum)

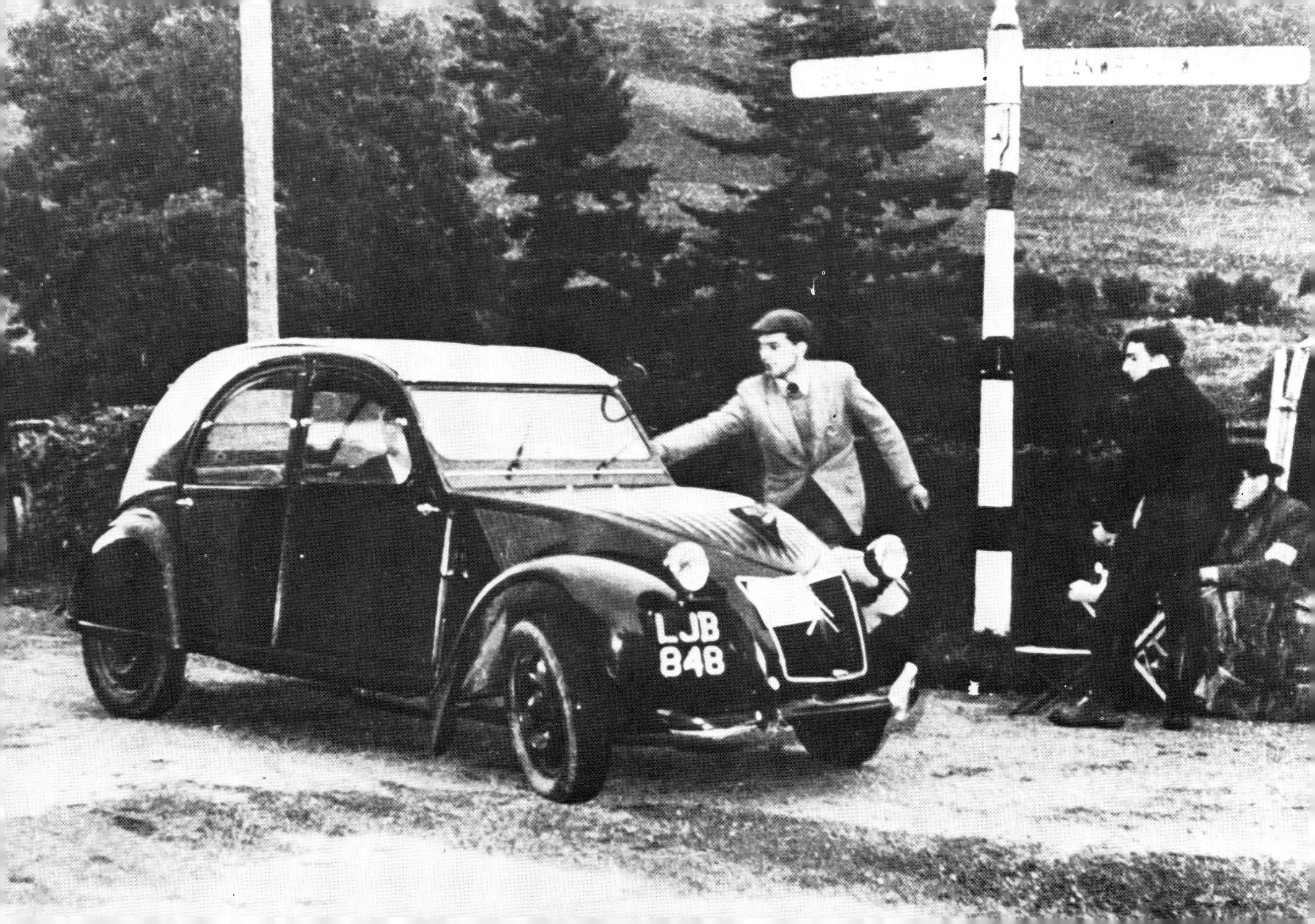
LJB
848

power output which employ heavy lumps of cast iron surrounded by water for engines, and I shall refuse to regard as an economy car any vehicle which does not give a genuine 60 miles per gallon of cheap grade petrol." Praise indeed from this highly critical savant.[1]

The road test in the now defunct *Light Car* praised the "unusually accessible" engine and gear box, the comfort of the seats and the Lockheed brakes. In summation is concluded; "At 60mpg the 2CV Citroën may well repay in fuel economy the import duty which makes the car somewhat costly in this country. Easy to drive, easy to park, economical to run, it is an unconventional but most acceptable answer to the modern motoring problem."

Almost in defiance of these glowing tributes the car refused to sell. Undeterred Citroën stepped up the publicity playing heavily on the car's growing reputation as a globe trotter and introduced the *fourgonnette* which had emerged to instant success on the continent in 1951. To further speed the sales a pick-up version, unique to Slough, was introduced and found a degree of favour with the farming community, (an interesting road test appearing in The *Farmers Weekly* of May 25, 1956), but found greater sales to The Royal Navy who used them aboard aircraft carriers as tractors and fitted them with recoiless 75mm guns as fast helicopter deployed assault vehicles for the Marine Commandos.

As late as 1955 these pick ups were appearing bearing 1953 chassis numbers. By this time both the cars, with the exception of the basic A models[2], and the vans had been fitted with the new 425cc 12bhp motor which had emerged in 1954 after the death of Boulanger who had steadfastly forbidden any increase in engine power or size on the grounds of increased danger.

The addition of a larger rear window for 1957 and a steel boot lid for 1958[3] did little to encourage sales so as a last despairing measure Citroën UK introduced a pretty glass fibre bodied coupé, reminiscent in some ways of the D5 range. This they called the *Bijou*. Unfortunately the high price and excessive weight coupled with the introduction of the all conquering Mini conspired together to defeat the project and the attempt to market the 2CV in Great Britain died.

---

[1] Motor Sport April 1954.
[2] See Appendix 1.
[3] British models had had a steel boot lid of sorts all along.

While the attempt to market the 2CV in Britain foundered the car went from strength to strength on the continent, becoming France's best selling car. Licensing agreements saw the car being produced in Argentina, Chile, Iran, Vietnam and Czechoslovakia. Interest having been aroused in the USA by favourable comment in *Road and Track* and the import of a few examples by francophiles led to an attempt to introduce the 2CV in commercial quantities in 1958.

"It's a safe bet that close on 10,000 Americans will buy the 2CV this year" enthused John Bentley in a road test in October's *Foreign Cars Illustrated* but he was slightly wide of the mark. Nowadays Citroën deny ever seriously trying to export the car to the States and, in an era of restrictive emission legislation, one can not only understand why but sympathise. Yet some still survive in the USA and a thriving club exists which, in 1982, hosts the latest raid.

Australia too was impervious to the charms of the little wonder car. In 1955 the influential magazine *Wheels* tested the 425cc car, complete with centrifugal clutch, and declared that in their opinion the only inhibiting factor to large scale sales in Australia was the utilitarian styling and price. Loaded as it was by freight and shipping charges, plus prohibitive tariffs, the car was simply not a bargain. In all some two hundred right hand drive 2CVs were sold in the middle to late fifties in Australia and, as in the States, some have survived and a club exists to cater for them.

The official reason given by the factory for withdrawing the 2CV from the British market has always been to maintain that the restrictive seat belt legislation made the car illegal. This fortunately did not deter those who wanted a 2CV from importing them from the continent. Indeed the importation of used examples became good business, as anyone who bought one from such people as Portobello Motor Company will attest. Here, for £150 upwards, a 2CV suitable for joining the posing elite of the Kings Road could be purchased and here they returned as the non mechanical owners poured water into the oil filler or failed to find the hiding place cunningly devised to keep the points from prying fingers such as theirs.

Perhaps unfortunately for Citroën those same people just could not be persuaded to accept the *Ami 6*. This ungainly monstrosity was first introduced to this country in 1966 having been on sale for three years in its native France. To the British who had accepted the badly built, agonisingly uncomfortable and abysmally styled Ford 105E Anglia the low performance and even ghastlier styling of the *Ami* rendered it a non starter in the sales race.

The sales performance of the *Dyane*, introduced in Britain only in its 602cc form in 1968, did little to further the career of the Citroën twins in this country, although at last the car's road performance, in terms of speed and acceleration, were falling more into line with what the driving populace wanted. Gaining acceptance as a smart and economical second car was about the limit of the *Dyane's* success until the petrol crisis of 1973-4.

This same crisis, coupled with the ever rising flood of privately imported continental examples, finally convinced Citroën to reintroduce the 2CV to Great Britain. Wisely the 602cc version now known as the 2CV6 was the only version made available and at once the motoring press began to pick up where the eulogies of the first introduction were left off.

"So much more value than just two horses", began John Bolster in his road test for *Autosport* in November 1974, before going onto detail the effectiveness of the measures adopted by Citroën to reduce interior noise in the car. These included anti-drum coatings on the front floor and bulkhead, a thick fibre blanket type lining for the bonnet, foam insulation for the heater ducts and a modified plastic cooling fan. He went on to point out the virtues of the demountable rear seats and the canvas roof which, although it was originally intended to facilitate the type of overloading Boulanger felt its agrarian and utilitarian life would inflict upon it, nevertheless provided a more than adequate full length sunroof.

"It is interesting that the two cylinder Citroën engines have been modified to pass the most severe European anti-pollution laws without any loss of performance or economy," he pointed out, before praising the cornering power and the well chosen gear ratios, ending his test with the words "...this must be one of the most important cars I have tested for *Autosport*."

Summing up a test in which economy, braking, accommodation and ride comfort drew generous measures of praise, *Motor* (November 30th 1974) enumerated thus. "FOR: very economical to run; good ride; generous accommodation; excellent sunshine roof; powerful brakes; cheap to buy. AGAINST: indifferent heating system; poor first gear synchro; awkward gear change; underdamped undulations."

Autocar (8th March 1975) pointed out that until the previous year Citroën had felt the car lacked appeal for reasons of snob value. Perhaps attendance at a few

Hampstead parties or a cruise through some of the back streets of Chelsea would have disencumbered them of that notion, however they went on to say; "Even now we are not offered the basic 2CV with its bench front seat and 425cc engine. Our 2CV has the 602cc engine which produces not 24 but 28.5bhp (at a remarkable 6,750rpm)". They also added that the intelligent Citroën driver husbands momentum and takes a run at any steep hill, presumably for anyone who couldn't decipher the power to weight ratio.

Judging the time right, Citroën took the opportunity to introduce 2CV Cross to the UK. Relieved of the high price which had originally disqualified it and fortified by the social acceptance of a new age of austerity, the car finally gained its rightful place in the market.

Below: Slough built AU of 1955 vintage pictured at the end of its working life in 1980. Note the bonnet insignia emblem – the wording was Citroën Front Drive, and the housing for the semaphore type trafficators. (Bob MacQueen)

Above: The 1954 Belgian built 2CV De Luxe added such nice little touches as a metal luggage boot, hub caps and extra chrome trim with rear side lights adapted from the Traction. Note the trapezoidal rear window. (Bob MacQueen)

Left and below: The introduction of the Dyane in 1967 brought the philosophy of the 2CV into a more acceptable package for the British market. These are the original Citroën publicity pictures. Note the four light coachwork not often seen in this country. (Citroën)

CITROEN

FRONT WHEEL DRIVE.

5 cwt. Light Van.

'2CV'

Offered on the chassis of the well-known '2CV' Citroen this Van makes an immediate appeal to all vehicle users where economy of operation is of vital importance.

The roomy body, low build, with flat floor, wide opening rear doors, and a loading space of 66 cubic feet, is ideal for the carrying of goods of all description.

The very soft suspension enables articles of a delicate nature to be carried without the need for special packing.

Petrol consumption 47 to 57 miles per gallon, at an average speed of 25 to 30 M.P.H.

The characteristics of Road Holding and Safety are as outstanding as those of the Saloon.

Unladen weight 10-cwt.   British Tax £10 per annum.

Maximum load 5-cwts. with driver.

Dimensions

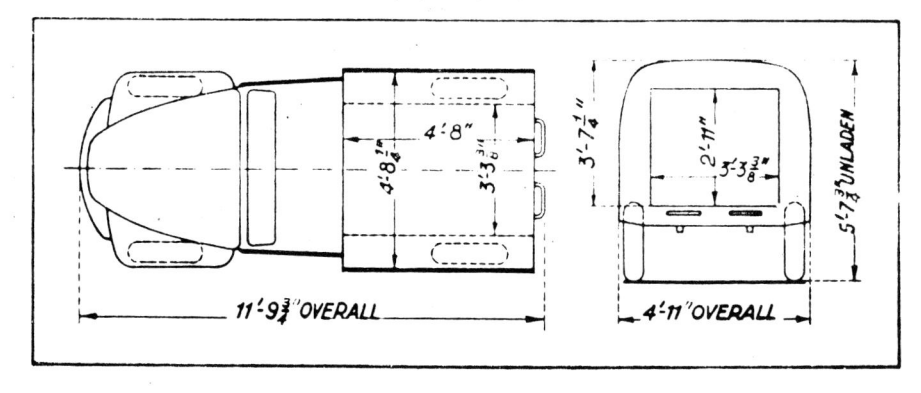

Citroen Cars Limited, Trading Estate, SLOUGH, Bucks.

Opposite: The first British sales brochure for the fourgonnette. (Reproduction represented as original)

Left: Social acceptability. Racing driver and journalist Tony Dron conducts his 1975 example complete with BARC badge and paddock pass through the infield at Silverstone. Although at six foot seven he's no midget, Tony didn't always steer with his knees. (Maurice Rowe)

Above: 1955 Slough built pick-up awaiting restoration in Cheltenham, 1981. (Bob MacQueen)

7 Cross Country 2CVs

Whilst the intrepid adventurers drove their 2CVs across the worst terrain the world could provide, some stirrings among certain Citroën agents began to make ripples at the factory itself. As a publicity stunt a few agents in the south of France had constructed twin engined 2CVs. The groundswell of opinion in the factory was that there might just be a market for more of the same which would solve the problem of what to do with the Panhard design team who had just been aquired along with their parent company.

As in 1936, the man chosen to ascertain the market was Duclos and his report was favourable enough for the factory to begin work on the prototypes in mid 1955. Working separately, the Citroën and the Panhard teams built their respective ideas of the project in the form of two prototypes from each company. The project was given the code name of A.W. (this was presumably before de Gaulle started banning English and its abbreviations from the sacred tongue) and these were duly shipped off to the French army testing grounds at Fontainebleau.

The result of this fusion of ideas was finally introduced to the European press at La Mer de Sable, virtually a miniature desert tucked away in the Forêt de Compiègne about 30 miles north-east of Paris. The car now boasted a dry weight of some 650 kilos (1,430 lbs) with a near as dammit 50/50 distribution of weight, a figure which the encroachment of the second engine gearbox and petrol tank helped to maintain as more or less constant.

By trial and error the suspension had been standardised to that of the basic fwd car whilst most of the equipment fitted a standard; for example oil bath air filters and lengthened undershield with strengthened bumpers, were lifted straight from the PO[1] models. In order to facilitate the two engines symmetricality about the car's transverse axis however, the rear engine was turned through 180 degrees

---

[1] These were models available in specially hostile export markets only.

Opposite: *Publicity photos of the original Sahara. (Citroën)*

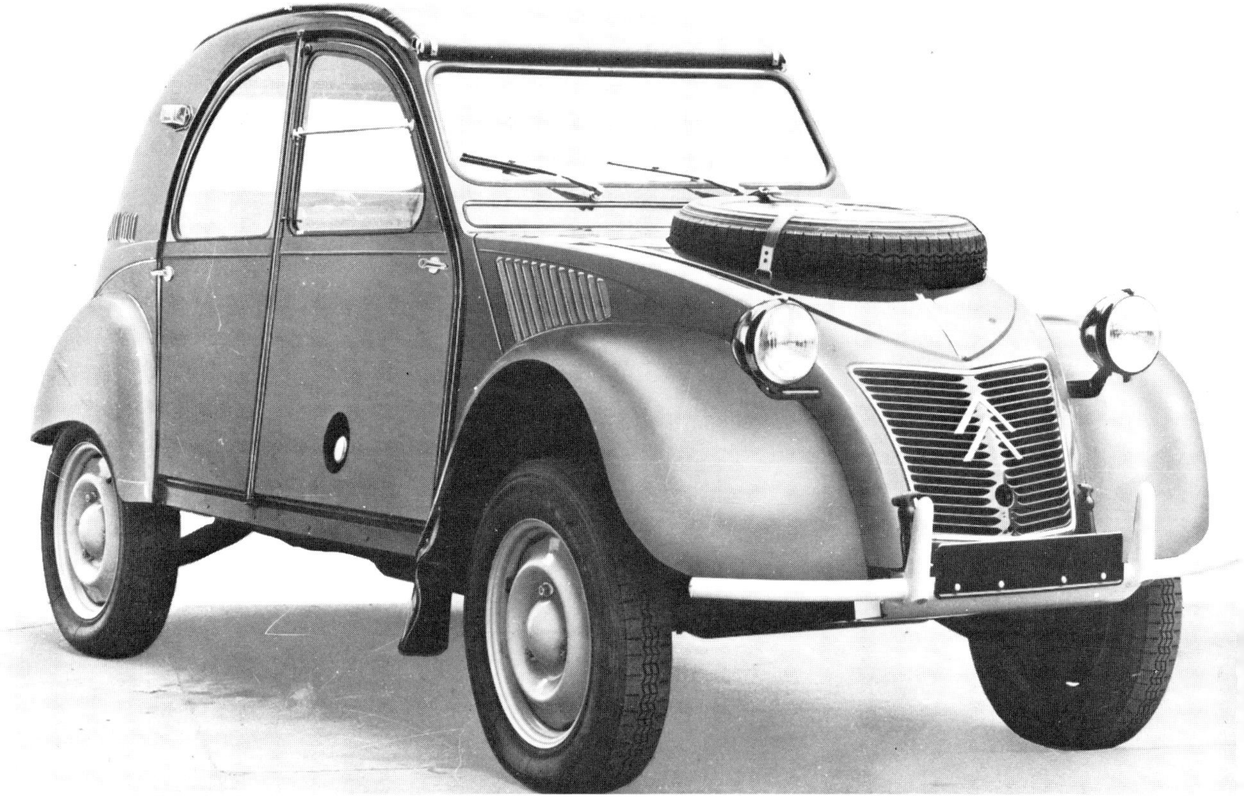

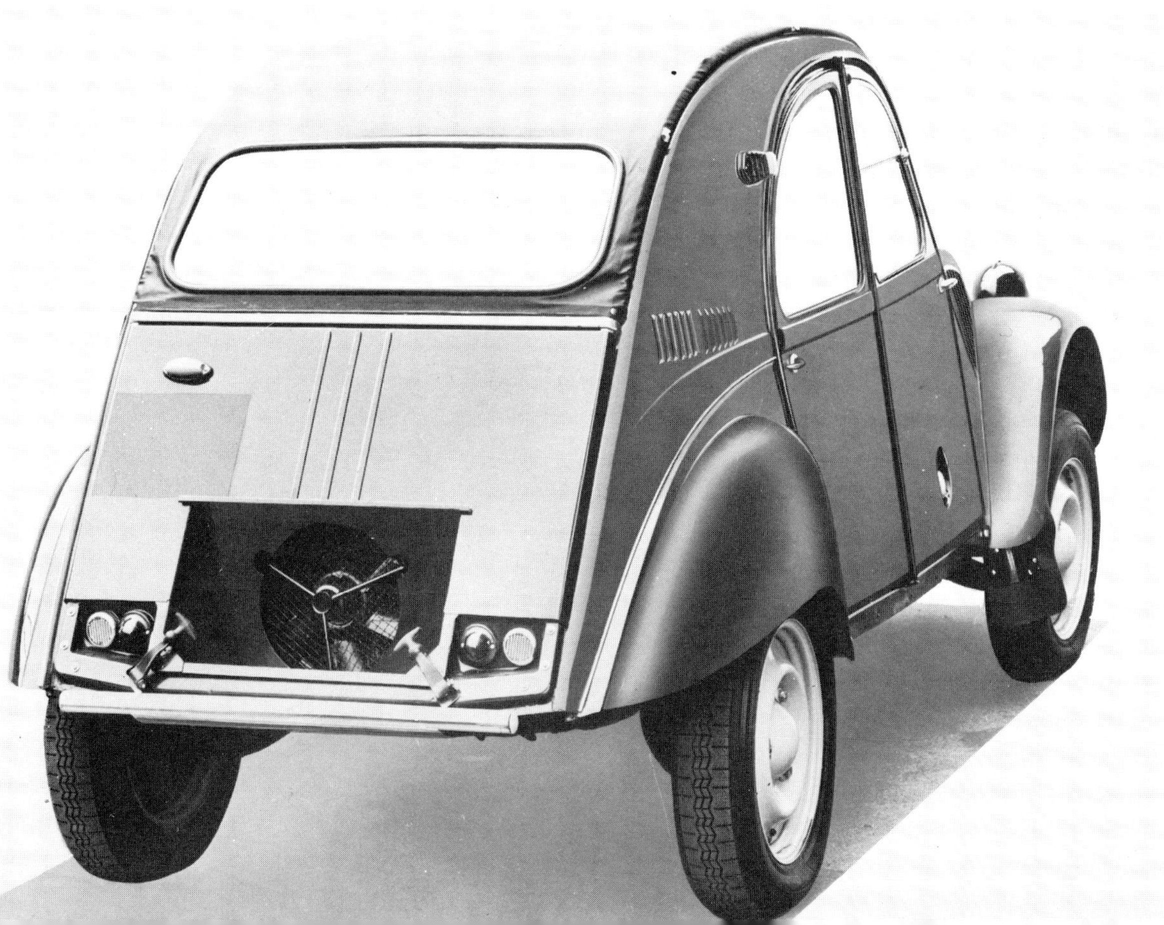

horizontal and the final drive crownwheel was placed on the opposite side of its driving pinion to give reversed rotation.

In normal cruising the car was in fact set up to use only the front engine, driving the front wheels in conventional style. The problems of rear engine inertia and single source all wheel drive being simply overcome by the use of the centrifugal clutch which naturally precluded the engagement of any of the gears in the rear box if the rear engine was not running. To facilitate an uncomplicated means of simultaneous change on both boxes the gear lever was floor mounted.

As can be seen from our photos, the *Sahara* boasted some tin opener type surgery on the rear wings, the rear bonnet and the front door which had to be cut to give access to the petrol tank mounted beneath the front seat. Yet, overall, the car looked surprisingly like its more mundane sisters. Other changes included the louvres to allow the rear engine to breathe and the inversion of the rear brakes. All in all only about a thousand *Saharas* were built, (legend has it that the last one was built for two Australians who died in a car crash en route to collect it in Spain) which makes it a fairly sought after piece of equipment.

Ten years after the launch of the *Sahara*, in direct response to the massive success of the charismatic Mini Moke, came the *Mehari* (see chapter 5). Technically this was interesting for being the first car in France, if not Europe, made from heat formed ABS plastic. A mish mash of 2CV6 running gear with *Dyane* lights and instruments, the *Mehari* made friends wherever it appeared, being adopted by the French armed forces for situations unsuitable to the normal jeep. This military interest saw the introduction of the *Mehari* 4x4 in 1975. Unfortunately this is not a twin engined confection on the lines of the Mini Twin Moke but, in effect, a scaled down Land Rover with plastic rather than aluminium bodywork.

The last of the cross country 2CVs to emerge from the factory was the FAF Series. Aimed primarily for production in underdeveloped countries (the initials stand for *'facile a fabriquer, facile a financer'*) the chassis is once more that of the 2CV6, whilst the *Mehari* inspired open or closed coachwork is made in sheet steel and requires no heavy or capital intensive plant.

The FAF comes in six versions:

1) The FAF limousine (sic) 5 doors, 5 seats, 6 side windows of which 4 slide, steel roof and folding rear seat.
2) FAF Break: 3 doors, 5 seats, 4 sliding windows, opening

fabric roof, folding rear seat.
3) FAF Break Commercial: 3 doors, 5 seats (3 removable), 2 sliding side windows, opening fabric roof, steel side panels.
4) FAF Pick up: essentially a steel shelled Mehari with two seats and a metal cab.
5) FAF Patrouille 4x2: 4 seats with a fabric canopy top similar to Mehari.
6) FAF Patrouille 4x4: similar to above but with four wheel drive.

Cartoon taken from Citroën's house magazine for the Mehari 4 x 4

UNE MEHARI FORTE COMME 4 × 4

Dessin Téteau
(Citroën 12.230)

Above: the Belgian Van Clee Emmet. *(Fabien Sabates)*

Left: First publicity shot of Mehari. *(Citroën)*

2 HORSE CROSS

It started in Belgium as did so many things 2CV, eventually it spread across the whole of Europe sponsored by Total and Citroën. It, of course, is 2CV Cross and here are some of the pictures that go to prove just what really does constitute a motorised masochist...

(Citroën)

(Bob MacQueen)

(Citroën)

(Citroën)

(Fabien Sabates)

(Bob MacQueen)

(Citroën)

85

(Fabien Sabates)

(Citroën)

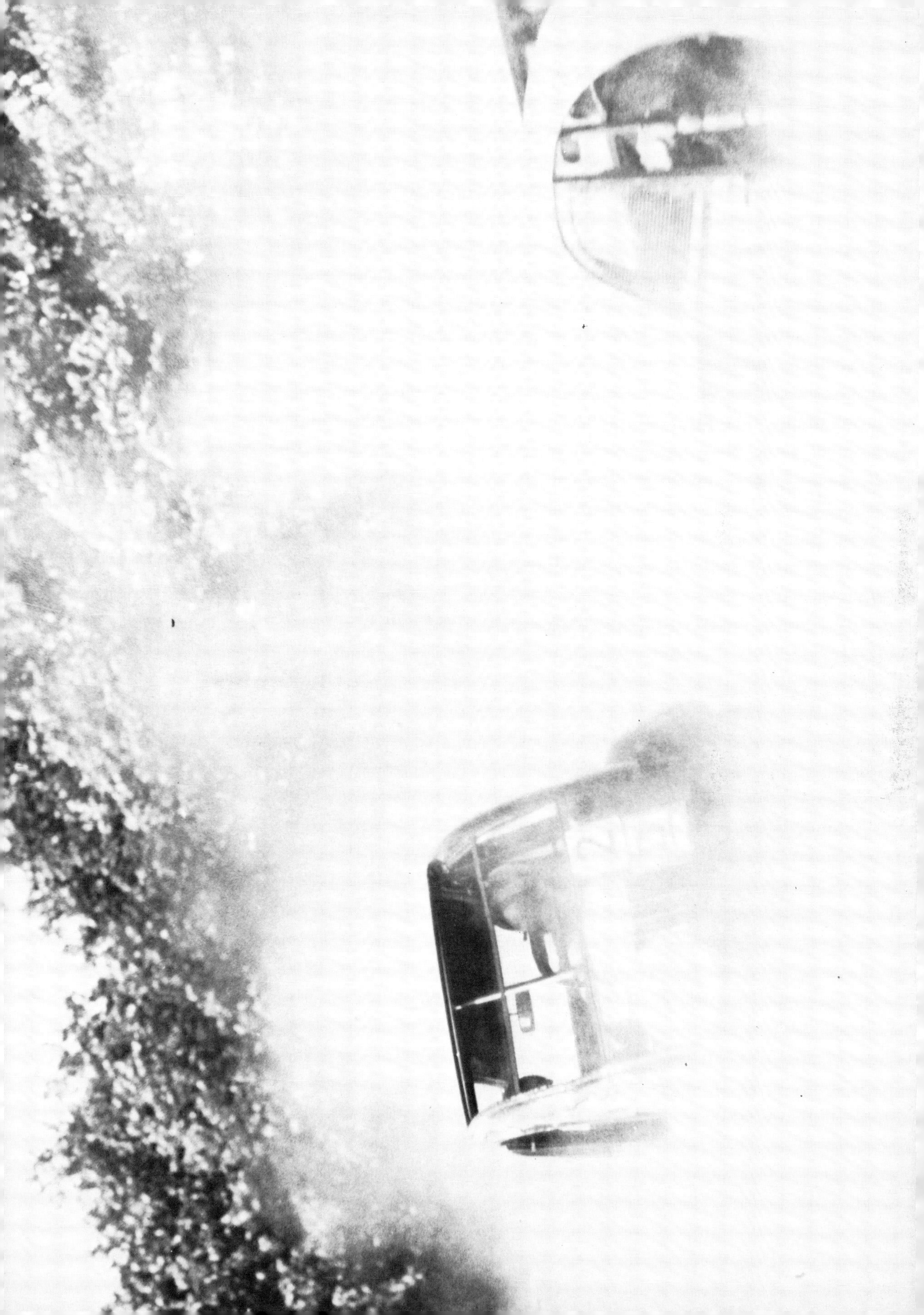

(Citroën)

(Citroën)

(Citroën)

(Citroën)

DUSTBINEERING

A truly English 2CV sport. Started by the Chelteham Flying Dustbin Preservation Society who use the soft muddy tracks through the Cotswolds for routes, dustbineering is part rally, part trial but mainly fun. Here the club are lined up on the first ever dustbineering foray.

Left: Hard line dustbineers waiting for the off in a Cotswold quarry. (Eric and Jackie Hatcher)

Above: Author Bob MacQueen dirtying his van. *(Bob MacQueen)*

Left: Halfway halt as chief dustbineer Martin marshals his followers. *(Martin Jones)*

Above: Typical dustbineers. (Bob MacQueen)

Left: Van – before the meeting. (Eric and Jackie Hatcher)

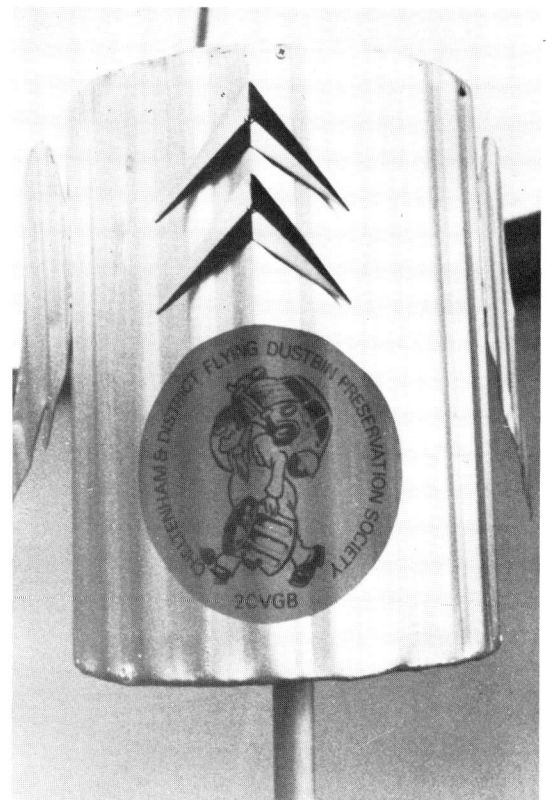

Above: At the end of the day, Cheltenham's very own fully automated car wash. (Martin Jones)

Left: The Flying Dustbin. (Martin Jones)

8 Further Developments

Although, with the emergence of the Sahara, the 2CV could be said to have reached its technical zenith, the rise of other vehicles such as the Renault 4 and the Mini, which offered more civilised accommodation and performance within the same price bracket, made it imperative that the car must change to fit the demands of the market. Thus, in 1961, by virtue of revamping the bonnet styling, fitting a new grille and replacing the traditional side louvres with longitudinal air intakes, the car was brought into line with current styling practice.

In Belgium six light coachwork had been available since 1956 and this became a feature of all export models except the most basic. A choice of colours was available, both in home and overseas markets, and the 425cc engine had been retuned to give 13.5bhp at 4,000rpm.

All through Europe the *fourgonnette* had made a name for itself by carrying the mails from the highest Alpine villages to the Flemish lowlands. This vehicle also got the benefit of the new bonnet and an improved range of colours whilst, in 1962, a new *commerciale* version of the basic car joined it in a quest to bring even more small business men into the 2CV fold. In reality this was more of a hatchback than a van but it at least countered some of the threat posed by the rival Renault.

By 1962 the *Ami 6*, introduced the previous year, had become France's best selling car. Nobody could have been surprised when the trend setting Belgian factory took the 602cc engine from this and added it to their six light body to produce the first 2CV6. So popular was this combination that in 1963 it was imported into France and in 1965 it was being built there. Also in 1963 the pleasant oval windows disappeared from the rear doors of the *camionette* to be replaced by more practical and much larger ones. Another welcome feature of the '63 models was the introduction of two rear brake lights on all French built models whilst the

Opposite: *Cutaway of the 1961 AZ. (Citroën)*

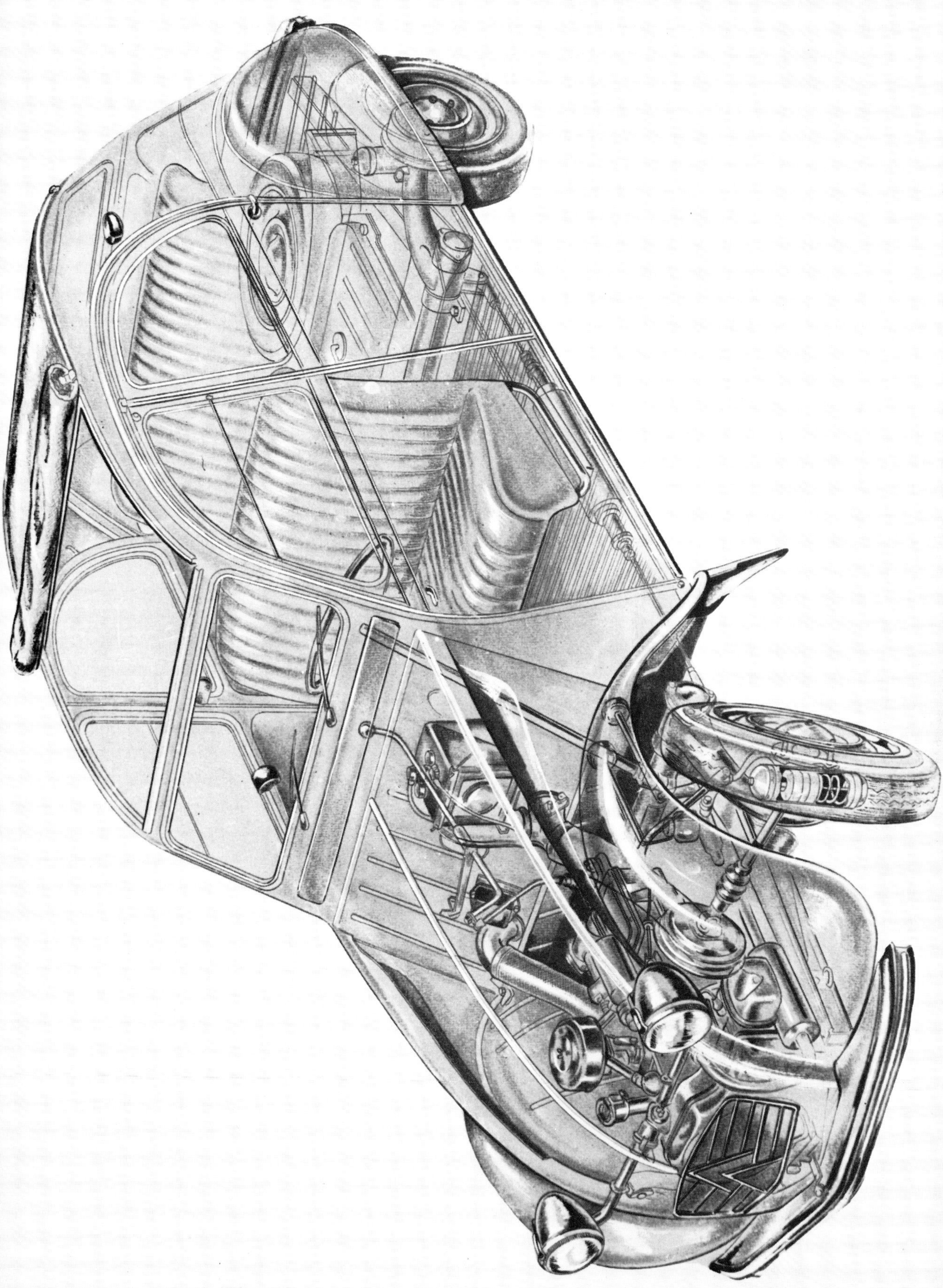

speedo finally assumed its rightful place in the driver's console and a fuel gauge added.

With safety legislation sweeping the world, 1965 saw the doors positioned so that they opened from the rear. The following year the first major change to Chinon's suspension was made when the car was fitted with hydraulic shock absorbers at the rear. This same climate of legislation brought about the fitting of three point seat belt mounting in 1972.

Ironically these changes were very much temporary measures for the philosophy at the factory in those days was purely to make the care more acceptable until the *Dyane* appeared to replace the aged 'duck'. With the demise of the *Dyane* in 1982 perhaps it may be seen that a certain sector of the motoring public prefers a car with no frills. Maybe even the Dyane was a little too pretty for the traditional 2CV customer and lacked the character that the new breed of owner wanted. However as from summer of 1982 only the Vigo plant in Spain will be making the *Dyane* and then only in its *Acadienne* guise.

Like its contemporary the VW Beetle the car has benefitted from constant updating; 1964 saw the adoption of tubeless tyres, 1966 the replacement of the 6 volt dynamo by a 12 volt alternator; in the time between constant velocity joints had replaced the original Cardan items. The major modification for 1967 was the addition of the instrument binacle from the *Ami 6* to the AZAM plus the incorporation of new door handles throughout the range whilst the vans acquired an entirely new gearbox.

Left: The fourgonnette with the new bonnet but still retaining the older windows at the rear. (Citroën)

Opposite: Poster advert from Yacco depicting Bardot and Vinatier 24 hour record for the 350cc class at Montlhery on 27 September 1953. (Huiles Yacco)

graissée avec
YACCO
La 2CV. CITROËN (350cmc) de l'Ingénieur Barbot
enlève le 27 Septembre 1953 à MONTLHERY
9 records internationaux
12 heures à 90,960 de moyenne
24 heures à 85,02 de moyenne

Above: 2CV6 engine prior to 1980 with single choke carburettor. (Citroën)

By 1970 the AZL had become the 2CV4 and acquired a new motor of 435cc giving 26bhp SAE at 6,750rpm and allowing 18.2kph in fourth gear. The 2CV6 boasted an engine uprated to give 33bhp SAE at 7,000rpm allowing 20.4kph per thousand revs in fourth and both cars sported the six light coachwork as standard. 1970 also saw the AKS 400 supersede the AK350 complete with 2CV6 engine, later to be joined by the AK250 as a 435cc replacement for the AZU.

By 1976 the cars had become so much more sophisticated than Boulanger's original that it was felt that a back to basics exercise was called for. The resultant car was the 2CV *Special*. Available only in the 435cc version in France to begin with, and fitted with the traditional four light bodywork, the car's success soon justified its launch into the export markets as well. Very soon the six light coachwork was restored, the 602cc motor became available and, to distinguish the level of trim, the more expensive versions took on the name of *Club*.

Unfortunately the inexorable march of progress has removed the vans from the catalogue but, as stated earlier, the Acadienne continues to be made and at present a healthy import trade is flourishing, albeit without the sanction of Citroën GB Ltd.

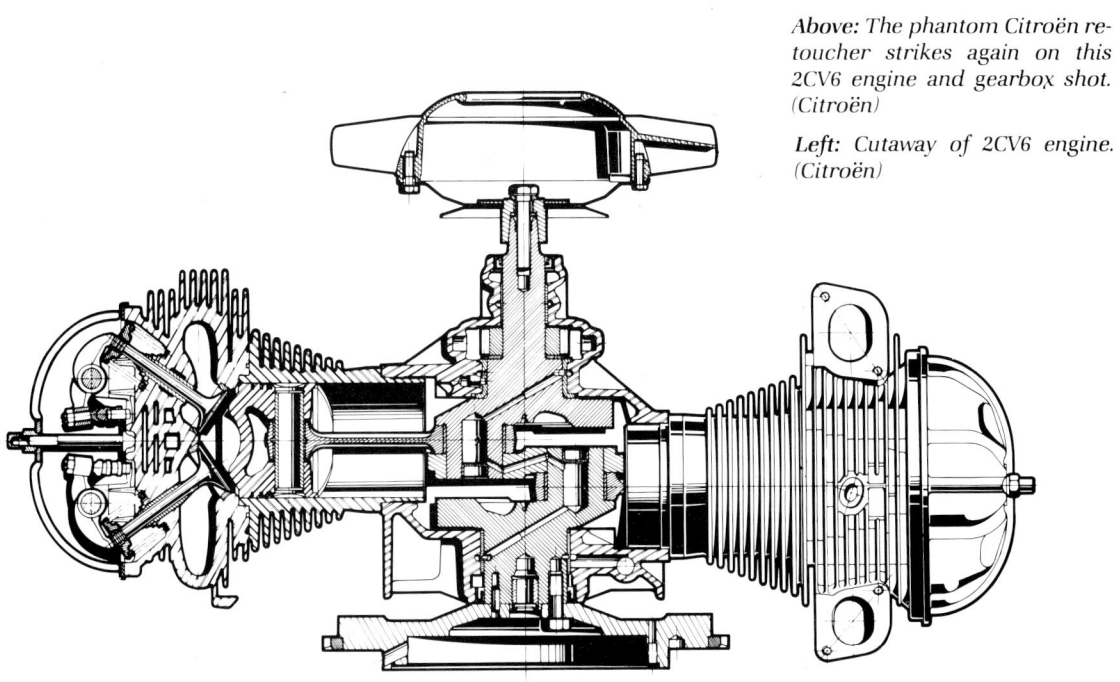

Above: The phantom Citroën retoucher strikes again on this 2CV6 engine and gearbox shot. *(Citroën)*

Left: Cutaway of 2CV6 engine. *(Citroën)*

Left: Dutch coupe de ville. (Peter Nunn)

Opposite top: Supreme paint job. (Peter Nunn)

Opposite below: Classic lines in this Belgian registered coupe. (Peter Nunn)

Below: 1955 Radar Coupe named after the constructor, M. Robert Radar of Liège. (Bob MacQueen)

PAINTING BY MARCUZZI
PHONE
032 41 32 55
CH

177
CITROBEL
AXT-878

Left: Ami 6 Estate. Not quite as hideous as the saloon. *(Bob MacQueen)*

Below: Ami 6 Saloon. Rare unrusted example caught at twilight. *(Bob MacQueen)*

9 Oddities

Left: Washing machine on the move. (Martin Jones)

Below: French micro fire engine. (Martin Jones)

The **CITROEN BIJOU** is unique in

104

THE UNIQUE CITROEN BIJOU

every way...

- for **comfort**
- for **safety**
- for **economy**
- for **simplicity**
- for **accessories**

and, of course, the BIJOU has
front-wheel drive
– a feature of all Citroen cars for over a quarter of a century!

The sales brochure for the Bijou, 1960.

Left: The famous log cabin. *(Bob MacQueen)*

Below: A French street scene. *(Martin Jones)*

Opposite above: Tasteful Swiss van interior. *(Bob MacQueen)*

Opposite below: Mercedes bonnet with rear extension snapped at Wagel. *(Bob MacQueen)*

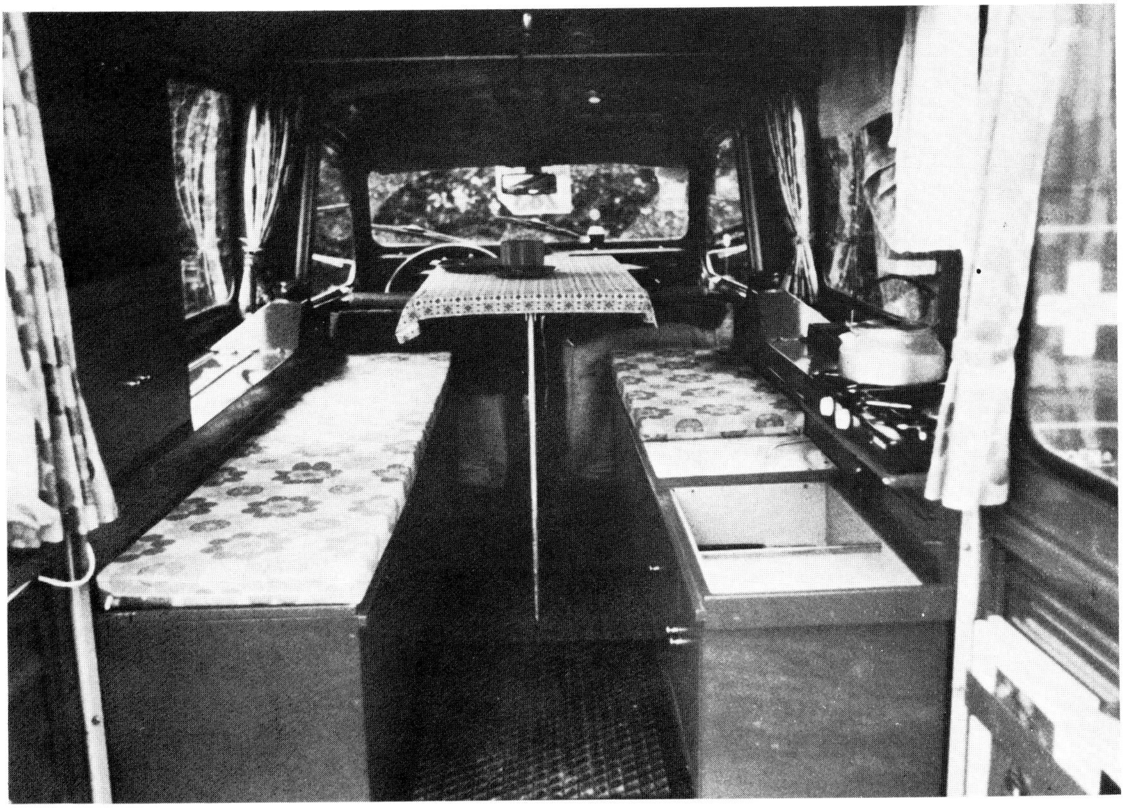

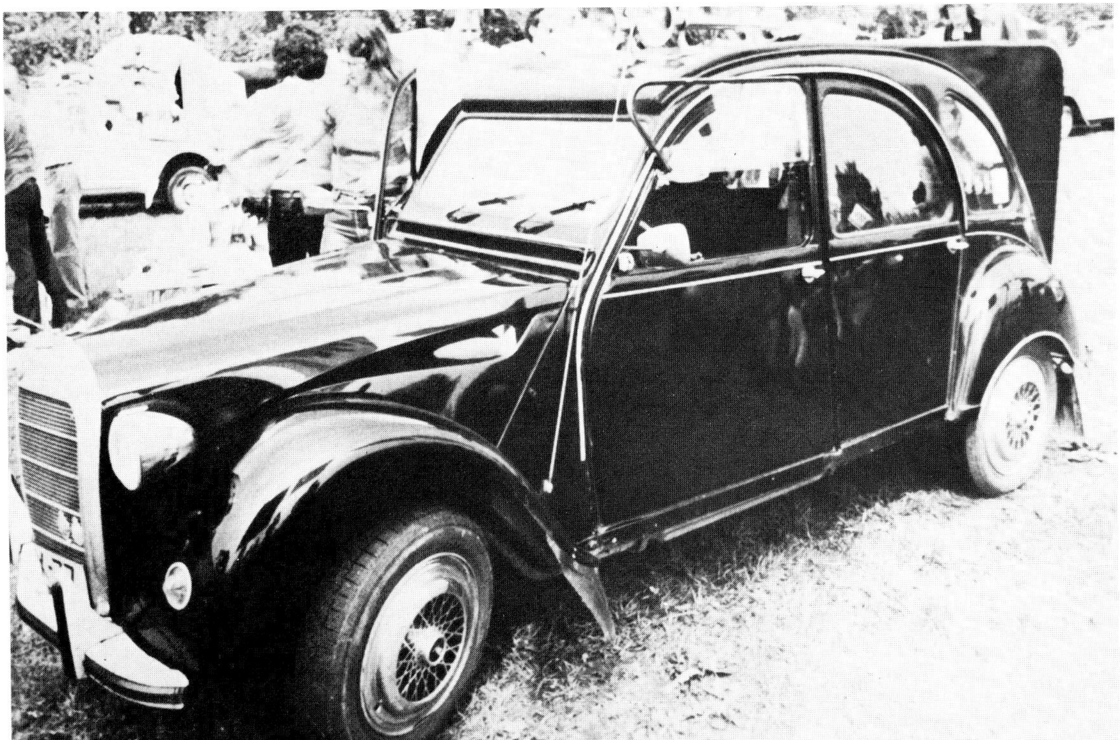

Left: "Four wheels, a platform and an umbrella" – PJB. *(Bob MacQueen)*

Below: Festive camper van. *(Bob MacQueen)*

Opposite: The ultimate in personalised cars. *(Bob MacQueen)*

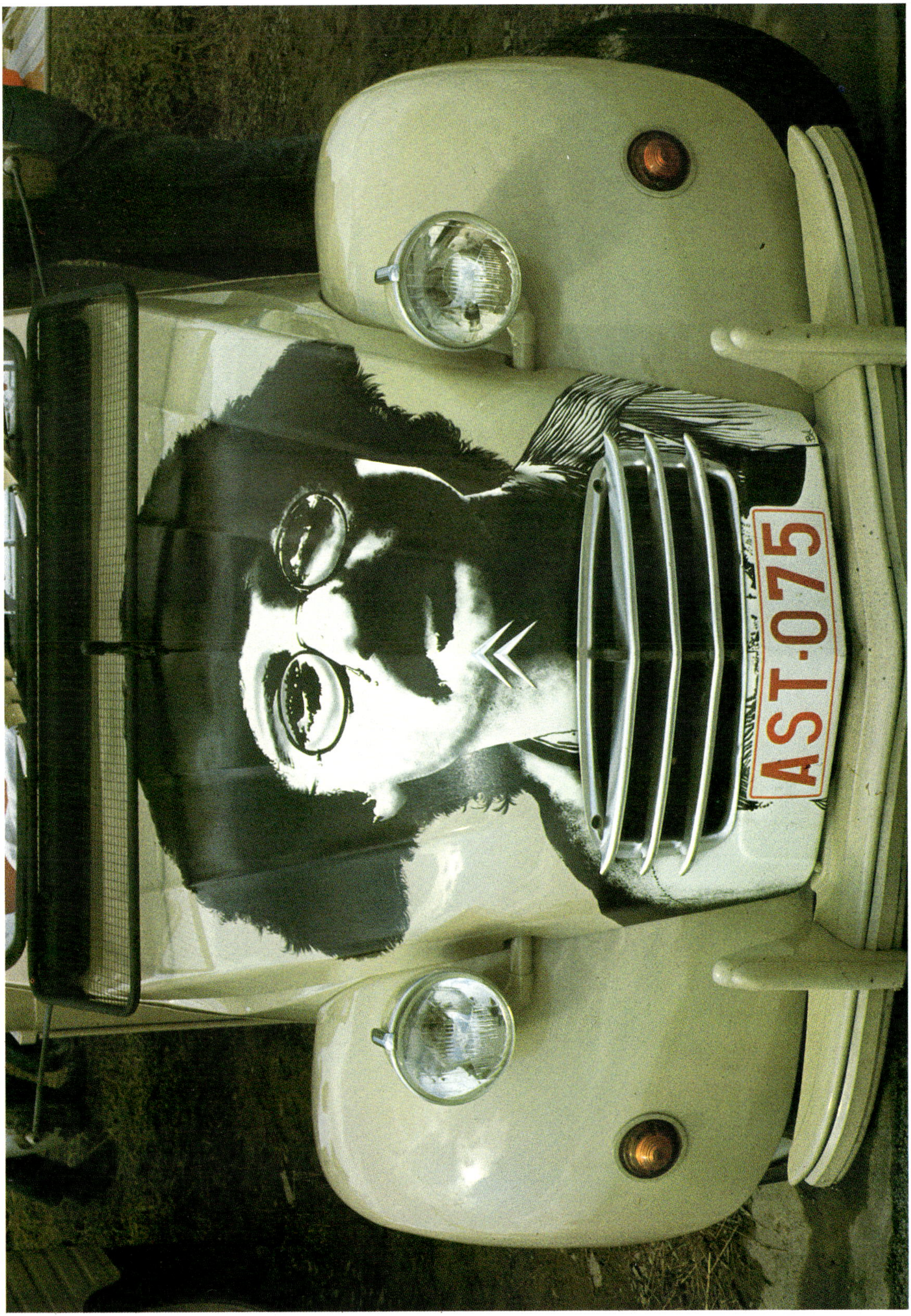
AST·075

Left: *Not really eight wheel drive is it? (Martin Jones)*

Above: *The authors' favourite. (Bob MacQueen)*

Opposite above: *The duck on the bonnet is remote controlled and squirts in any direction. (Bob MacQueen)*

Left: The beautiful St Tropez. *(Julien Vlaminck)*

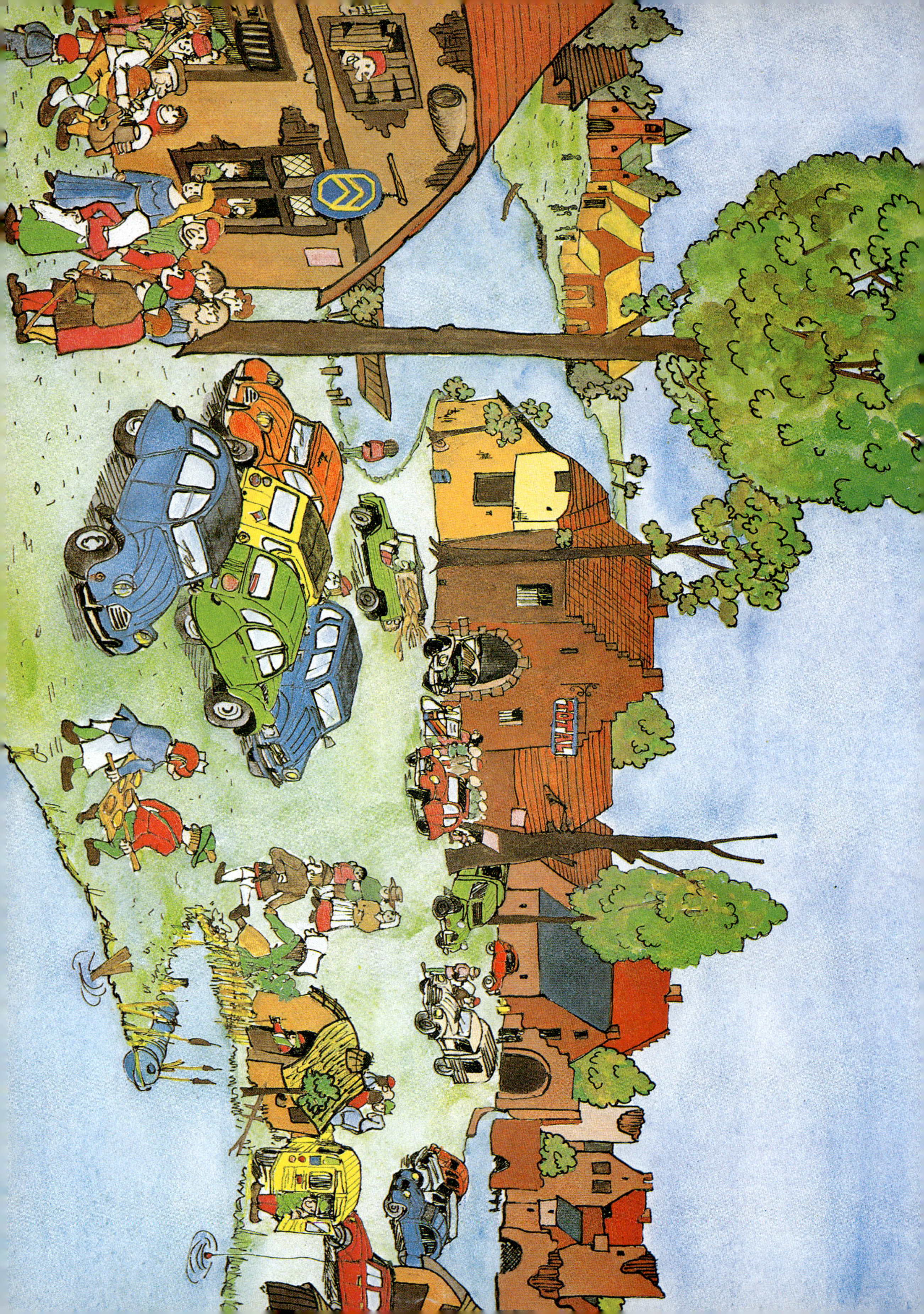

Opposite: Poster for 4th International meeting of 2CV Friends, Belgium, August 1981.

Left: Cuddly 2CVs. *(Bob MacQueen)*

Below: Pedal 2CV. *(Peter Nunn)*

Left: 2CV in a bottle. *(Citroën)*

Below: Vine spraying 2CV. *(Fabien Sabates)*

Left: Julian Vlaminck's pick-up. (Bob MacQueen)

Below left: Austrian built bonnet kit. (Citroën)

Below: Factory built taxi. (Citroën)

Left: 2CV buggy. (Citroën)

Above: Specially lightened 2CV. (Citroën)

Left: Desert mobile. (Citroën)

Opposite above: What can one say! (Citroën)

Opposite below: How the gentleman with the beard spent his weekends for a few years. (Bob MacQueen)

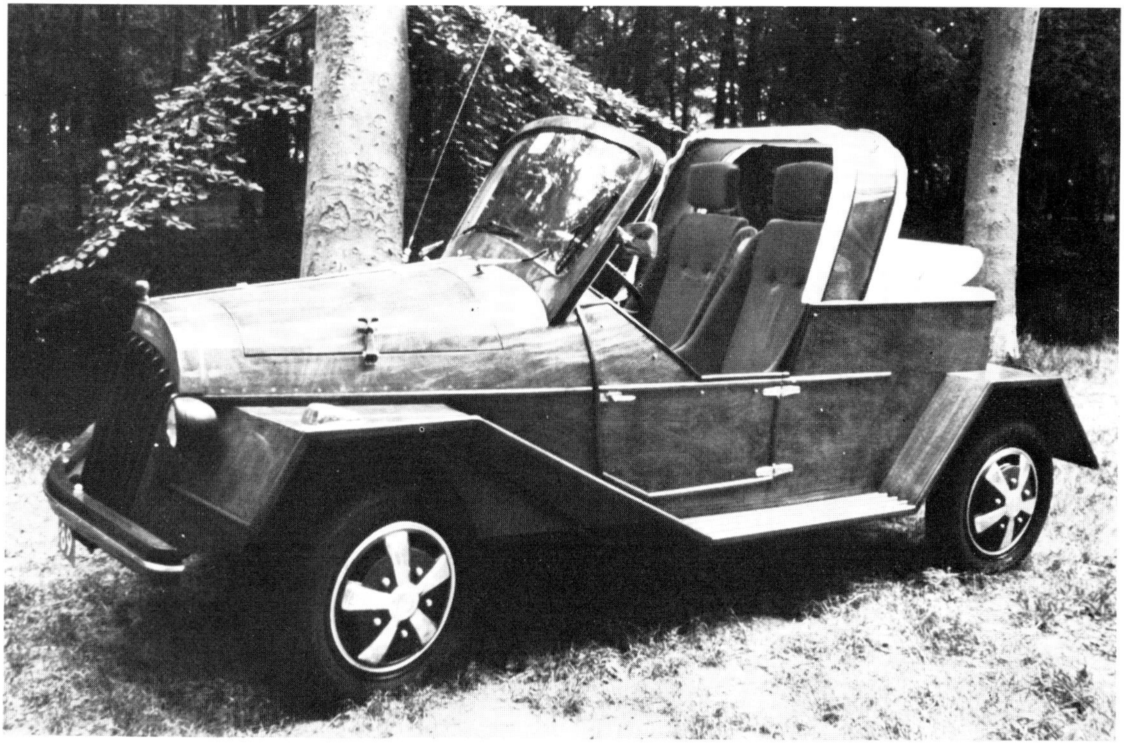

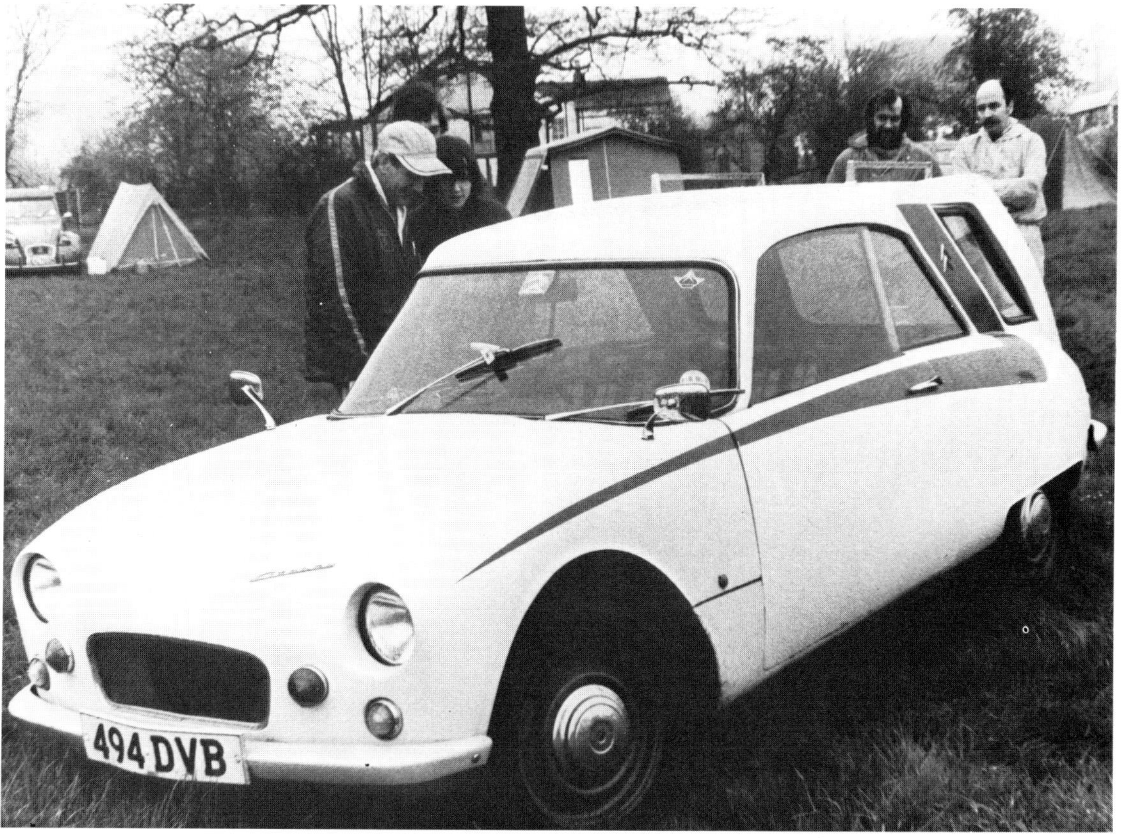
494 DVB

Left: What is it? (Peter Nunn)

Left: What might have been... a factory styling exercise from 1965. (Fabien Sabates)

Above: All done in the best possible taste... (Peter Nunn)

Left: The baseball boot. (Citroën)
Below: Fred arriving at Wagel. (Bob MacQueen)

Left: What do you mean Kubelwagen? German buggy variation. (Peter Nunn)

Middle left: Van complete with Triumph Vitesse running gear... (Peter Nunn)

Middle right: And France's reply! (Garage Régnier)

Bottom left: Claude's double decker and – right – the stove, which really works. (Bob MacQueen)

Above: Every one knows the Swiss are money conscious but there must be better ways to build an air force! (Citroën)

Left: Meanwhile, back in Britain they are still looking. (Citroën Car Club)

Below: Aquatic Kiwi! (Citroën Car Club)

Left and below: There is simply nothing ... like messing about in boats. (Citroën)

Above: It floats too, honest! (Citroën)

10 The Clubs

"There seems to be a definite 2CV cult in course of creation and an extraordinary spirit of camaraderie exists between owners."

The Autocar 27-2-1953

THE CLUBS

The rise of the 2CV clubs throughout Europe, and indeed the world, is a unique story. One make car clubs have existed for nearly as long as have cars but to find a one vehicle club in such large numbers so widely spread must be without parallel.

Nippon Club Citroën would appear to have been the first. It was formed in 1935 by the Japanese Citroën distributor to boost sales through camaraderie. Taking its cue from this venture the factory followed suite and, until the early sixties, Europe was dotted with factory founded clubs. In all probability the second club on the scene was the The Citroën Car Club founded in Great Britain in 1948. Here one of the first members was a merchant seaman who took to proselytising the club at each port of call with windscreen stickers, thus ensuring a world wide membership.

During the 50's and 60's the factory insulated purchasers and would be purchasers of the 2CV against the scorn of their fellows by funding clubs, where anyone demonstrating the type of insanity required to buy a 2CV could consult with fellow aberrationists. Germany, Holland, Denmark, Austria and Switzerland were among the countries so favoured and herein lay the foundation for the modern 2CV clubs which grew organically when the support of the factory was withdrawn.

In Belgium, Citroën were instrumental in founding the first club exclusively devoted to the 2CV in 1953. At its height the club boasted over a thousand members and produced a monthly magazine but the organization collapsed when Citroën Belge withdrew their support. The same happened in Switzerland.

In Holland during the early sixties Citroën gave away free plastic ducks to grace the rear windows of the 2CV and even went as far as producing a pop record to promote the car. This could well have been the origin of the nickname *'Het Lelijke Eendje'* (the ugly duckling) although in fairness it could have been inspired by it. Either way the name has stuck and today a good percentage of European clubs still feature the duck as part of their emblem. At this time (1965) the Dutch Citroën Company were circulating twenty thousand of their magazines a month. In turn the demand for parts and accessories in Holland led to the founding, in 1966, of a specialist shop called Paris Parts in Amsterdam thus instituting the means for customised ducks.

THE RAIDS

A prophet is not without glory save in his own country and in France 2CV clubs, if they existed, did so at a very low key. To raise the level of awareness Jacques Wolgensinger decided to bring a touch of adventure to the image by taking a lesson from André Citroën himself and emulating the spirit of his famous raids. These were thrown open to any owner between eighteen and thirty with a 2CV and were run under the patrimony of the French secretariat in charge of youth, sport and leisure.

The first raid was the Paris-Kabul in 1970 and the success of this brought about the Paris-Persepolis in 1971. In turn this brought about the greatest, which was almost a repeat of the *Croisière Noire, Le Raid Afrique,* of 1973.

Thirteen hundred people and five hundred 2CVs heeded the call of Afghanistan and followed the route to Kabul. The spirit and the low level of mechanical mortality were outstanding to say the least and a good proportion joined the trail, now sponsored by Citroën, Total, RTL and Iran House to Persepolis. This time, however, a selection form was sent out to would be entrants to test the drivers' ability to cope with a breakdown under strenuous circumstances and their ability to fix any breakages which might occur.

Participants were expected to report at Titograd, Salonika, Var, Mamachan, Istambul and Paris. The conditions of participation demanded that each crew keep a log of the journey on tape and film and the ten which were adjudged best were rewarded with new cars. The first prize was a brand new GS! Entrants comprised fifteen Spanish, twenty five Dutch, twenty five Germans, two Austrians, twenty five Belgians, two Danes, fifteen Italians, one Norwegian, two Swedes, twenty five Swiss, four Portuguese, five Jugoslavs and two Finns the remainder being French. Again the mechanical mortality rate was commendably low.

An acute attack of xenophobia seems to have afflicted the powers that be over the *Raid Afrique* for only French crews were allowed to compete. Still the pictures were nice....

Immediately (by French standards) after this a 2CV club sprang up in France in 1980.

In chronological terms the main upsurge in 2CV clubs seems to have begun in Denmark and Sweden, closely followed by Finland, Norway, Austria, Germany, Switzerland and Holland. These were the 'organic' clubs owing nothing to Citroën. The form that the clubs would take was more or less decided by the character of the cars themselves. The talk at the meetings is less of engines, gear boxes and modifications than of horizons waiting to be crossed, the price of beer at the last or next meeting and the good times to be had visiting fellow 2CVers in other climes.

As the president of the 2CV GB Club chooses to put it: "Why this is so I find hard to explain. Does the 2CV attract people of like minds or do you change when you buy a 2CV? I begin to believe a little of the latter; drive a 2CV and it will change your life! 2CV owners whilst being knowledgeable about the cars hardly treat them as status symbols; how could they – after all a 2CV is a 2CV...."

DANSK CITROENKLUB

The Danish Citroën Club was founded on the fourth of September 1956 when it was christened the 2CV Club of Denmark. The prime motivator was a clerk at Citroën who, with a few like minded friends, realised that owners of 2CVs in Denmark were having problems with technical matters. At the end of the first year membership had reached one hundred and the club began to make contact with other embryo organisations in other countries. It produced a monthly magazine which drew a small amount of backing from Citroën.

In 1960 the club was opened to all models and adopted its present name in 1963, by which time links had been forged with the other Scandinavian clubs. This allowed the production of what still must count as the most stylish and informative magazine to arise on the club scene. Called *Attraction* it continues to be published monthly with occasional special editions devoted to a particular Citroën model. Membership peaked at 650 in 1976 and the Club was host to the 3rd International meeting of 2CV friends in 1979.

Recently the club has split into two factions, Citroënisterne I Danmark and the original Dansk Citroënklub.

SVENSKA CITROEN KLUBBEN

Founded in 1958 as the Swedish 2CV Club the development closely followed that of the Danish club opening its doors to all Citroëns when, due to a regrettable oversight on the part of Citroën, no 2CV was available with headlight wipers, rear seat belts, plastic coated brake pipes or emission controls necessary to meet Swedish safety regulations. Some hardy individuals still manage to import the odd 2CV into Sweden but the majority of models in the club are perfectly preserved pre-1966 models. Present membership is about 600 members including a few Panhards.

NORSK 2CV KLUB

Two dozen 2CVs fought their way through a blizzard to start the club in 1965 at a restaurant. At that time the 2CV was considered a very strange beast and definitely not the thing to have in the driveway! As membership grew the club split into local organisations including the Polar Circle 2CV Club the most Northerly club in the world. There are at present some three hundred members, who have their own club house where monthly meetings are held. Once a year the Club organises a trip for orphans to some place of interest. The Club contributes to the production of *Attraction* and considers its primary function to be liaison with overseas clubs.

FRATERNITAS SANCTI ANDREAS (FINLAND)

This club, founded in 1962, is perhaps the most intriguing of all the 2CV clubs. It is a closed society restricted to owners of A models only. If any member sells his car his membership is automatically withdrawn. The prime rule of the club is "The 2CV is everything, everything for the 2CV". All members are equal except at the annual ball where members are ranked as Honorary Master, Master, Journeyman and Apprentice. The latter having no vote.

An Apprentice is a new member who has yet to own his 2CV for one year or 15,000 kilometers. When these conditions are met the Apprentice can become a Journeyman, after an initiation ceremony at the annual ball. To rise to the rank of Master the Journeyman has to serve humbly for two years whilst driving 30,000 kilometers. An Honorary Master attains his status by driving 75,000 kilometers in his 2CV.

The Club boasts over two thousand members, split into twenty seven regional groups, plus an independent club in Helsinki. Events organised include ice races and rallies plus sauna meetings. In 1975 the club organised the first international meeting of 2CV Friends drawing people from twelve countries in four hundred cars. At the second meeting in 1977 fifty Finnish cars made the long trip to Switzerland. The club publishes its own magazine eight times a year and its main aim is not to increase membership but "to improve the quality of happenings and find the best possible harmony in the funny life we lead."

The club also produce a booklet called *APUA!* or Help which lists members of the 2CV clubs throughout the world who will give assistance to stranded 2CV drivers.

In exchange for being listed a subscriber receives a copy of the book so he too can partake in this brilliantly altruistic scheme.

HOLLAND

In Holland there is no national 2CV club although a Citroën club does exist. Local clubs however, proliferate, with perhaps the best known internationally being the Waggel Club of Rotterdam. This was founded in 1975 and the name means literally 'waddle' which takes us back to the plastic ducks given out by the agents in the sixties. The name of the club is reflected by the names of individual cars such as 'Lucky Ducky' or 'Pink Duck' and customisation of both cars and H vans runs high.

Since May 1976 the club has hosted an annual international meeting which grows in size every year attracting over four hundred cars from all over Europe in 1982.

Other clubs include 2CV Club Grootebroek and the 2CV Hillbillies.

BELGIUM

With the death of the original Citroën funded club in 1957 the club scene in Belgium lay dormant until 1974 when the 2CV-Dyane Club Belge was formed. It remained fairly small until 1978 when an international meeting to celebrate the thirtieth birthday of the 2CV at Rochefort put the Club well and truly on the map. The 1981 meeting of the Friends of the 2CV was held, by all who attended, to have been a huge success and under the leadership of Julien Vlaminck the Club is active both socially and technically. Julian himself had nine versions of the 2CV when last counted including a rare *Radar*, an *Emmet* and a delectable *Sahara*.

GERMANY

The main German Citroën Car Club was formed in 1960 but the national 2CV club became an offshoot in 1971. The first 2CV club seems to have been centred upon Frankfurt and produced a magazine called *Töff*. From the very earliest days German 2CV clubs have tended to be small regional organizations and no real co-ordinating body exists for them. The Citroën Club Rhine Ruhr carries news from many clubs. Other clubs include 2CV club Duisberg, Citroën Club Celle, Citroën Club Koln, and the Moin/Moin Norden. The German club members are great travellers, a large contingent making a welcome presence at most international meetings. The fifth international meeting of 2CV Friends is due to be held in Germany in July 1983.

AUSTRIA

Under the umbrella of the Osterreichischer-Citroën-Club some dozen or so 2CV clubs thrive in Austria. Since 1972 the national club has produced a fine monthly magazine.

SWITZERLAND

Like Austria the Swiss have a national organisation which publishes a monthly newsletter named *Doshwo-zietung*. There are between eighteen and twenty clubs operating on a regional level throughout Switzerland, three from the French speaking canton, one from the Italian and the rest German. Like the Germans the Swiss are great travellers and cut a stylish dash at internationals with their cars drawn up about the Swiss flag.

FRANCE

Until very recently the homeland of the 2CV was the least distinguished in terms of clubs. Just why this should be so is something of a mystery when the French are as fanatical as anyone else about the 2CV. However, in late 1979, a 2CV club was formed in St Etienne 2CV Club Forizien, which at present boasts twenty two members.

PORTUGAL

At least one club exists in Portugal as one car arrived at the international meeting in Belgium.

CZECHOSLOVAKIA

The 2CV was sold in Czechoslovakia for a number of years but is no longer available thus there are problems with spares. The club was formed some years ago to help members with spares. Occasionally a Czech will get out to an international meeting but severe restrictions mean that they cannot hold meetings themselves.

YUGOSLAVIA

The Cimos factory produces *Dyanes* from knock down kits but in the past it did produce 2CVs. The Yugoslav club factory backed and has hosted meetings.

USA

The Deux Chevaux Club USA does in fact exist. It was started by an ex-pat Brit named Richard Bonfort who arrived in the US in a 2CV van. There are a fair number of 2CVs in the States most of them grouped about the West Coast. The 2CV was at one time available in the USA, the price for the 1956 model being quoted at $1,145 on the Eastern seaboard. It appears to have been available up until 1960 although no sales figures are available. A few 2CVs trickle into the States still but these, by law, are required to be earlier than 1967 or to have the full emission control system, five mph bumpers etc. etc. For 1982 the club has organised a coast to coast drive with a convoy of 2CVs from all over Europe

AUSTRALIA

The Coo-ee Whoopee Bonzer Club is based in Victoria. Three intrepid members arrived in England in 1980 and demonstrated the typical Aussie charm and resilience in the face of alcohol over and above the call of normal drinking. Great guys.

GREAT BRITAIN

At the time of writing there are four major clubs in the UK, the oldest being the North Eastern 2CV Enthusiasts club. This is a small group based in Newcastle Upon Tyne and formed in the early seventies. The largest club is the 2CVGB club which was formed in March 1978 by a group of twenty four 2CV enthusiasts who broke away from the Citroën Car Club. For some years previous to this there had been a separate group within the CCC called 2CV Friends and these had begun to liaise with various overseas clubs and make the odd journey to foreign meetings.

In 1976 the CCC played host to the third International Citroën Car Clubs Rally. Amongst the overseas clubs who attended were the Waggel Club from Holland who made many converts to the AK van and its easy conversion to a camper. The residual interest left by the various foreign clubs and the need to maintain closer contact with the overseas outfits was thus a major factor in the setting up of 2CVGB which had its inaugural meeting at The Oak in Leamington Spa. It was envisaged from the start that the ideal set up for the club would be along the lines of the Danish club with regional clubs maintaining the interest at a grass roots level and various clubs began to form quite quickly.

In September 1978 the mid Wessex Club was formed followed almost immediately by the London Boozers. In November 1978 the Cheltenham and District Flying Dustbin Preservation Society was set up, this in turn being followed by the Godiva Two Horse Riding School from Coventry and the Camel Club from Essex. CV Ecosse spread the club to Scotland and within four years there were eighteen local clubs.

One of the first concerns of the infant club was the organisation of an international meeting on the Essex Show ground combined with a 2CV Cross meeting. The whole event was a resounding success with cars arriving from Holland, Belgium Denmark, Germany and the whole of the UK. So successful was it that the international has continued to be run on an annual basis, growing in size every year.

The club publishes a monthly magazine *2CVGB News* which carries articles of technical interest as well as travel and anecdotal articles. From this has sprung the *Help* booklet modelled on the Finnish *APUA* listing all who are willing to come to the aid of a fellow 2CVer in distress. Another recent innovation is the register for the older types of 2CVs in the country to assist in maintaining a steady supply of the more innaccessible spares. Other British clubs not affiliated to 2CVGB include the 2CV Club Cornwall and the Wessex 2CV Club.

THE INTERNATIONAL MEETINGS

From their first foundations the main function of the 2CV clubs has been that of organising social functions. From the meetings grew the weekends where like minded and amiable 2CV nuts could pitch their tents and share their camaraderie into the early hours. Occasionally semi humourous competitions would take place and traditionally a concours. In 1973, with the first International Citroën Car Club Rally, the meetings took on an international aspect. The success of the original Yugoslavian meeting established The ICCCR as a biennial event. Other venues have been Vienna '74, Britain '76, France '78 and Holland in '81.

Although the 2CV representation at these events has always been fairly strong the dominant feature of these gatherings has been the older and more respectable cars which comprise the exhibits at the concours events. Thus, with the emergence of the 2CV clubs, the principle was naturally adopted as soon as liaisons had been established.

The first 2CV Friends International was held in 1975 in Finland attracting over one hundred cars from all over Europe. The relaxed attitude and friendly informality of this meeting happily set a precedent for the subsequent meetings. Obviously the cars are discussed but usually such matters only arise when a participant decides to change an engine or even perhaps a body!

The biennial meetings usually run over three days. There are flea markets where everyone has the chance to buy or sell 2CV artifacts, competitions such as jousting where two cars are driven towards each other and the passengers standing on the front seats pelt each other with cream pies. There is usually a procession and the sort of nutty games which feature in the lighter moments of *Jeux Sans Frontières*.

The main events for the 2CV friends have so far taken place were in Switzerland in '77, Denmark in '79, Belgium, where a special unscheduled meeting for the cars 30th birthday had already been organised in '78, hosted in '81 and Germany has the honour in 1983. Attendance has risen to a massive 3,000 2CVers from (at the last meeting) twenty two countries, driving 1,500 cars.

Below: The Aussie Club on parade (left) plus an 'H' van and 2CV down under.

INTERNATIONAL CLUB ADDRESSES

AUSTRIA, Gunter Jung, Waldgasse 39, 1100 Wien

AUSTRALIA, Phil Ward, 15 Gluyas Avene, Grance 5022

BELGIUM, Julien Vlaminck, Labbelaan 10, B 1900, Overijse

CZECHOSLOVAKIA, Hula Lubomir, Sana Zelivskeho 29, 1300 Praha 3

DENMARK, Claus Jacobsen, Prs. Alexandrines, 2920 Charlottenlund

Gert Jensen (Dansk Citroënklub), Heimalsgade 60, 9000 Aalborg

FINLAND, Teemu Eerola, Kelohogantie 20, 15200, Lahti 20

FRANCE, Christian Police (2CV Club Forizien), 4 Rue Des Jasmins, Meythet 74000

WEST GERMANY, Guntram Bergman (CCRR), Neckarstr 54, D-4300 Essen, 18-Kettwig

EAST GERMANY, Both Istvan, 8142 Radeberg, Forststrasse 23

HOLLAND, Fred Langhorst (2CV Club Waggel), Ruivendwarsstraat 146, 3036 Db Rotterdam

W.V. Gool (2CV Billies), Tramsingel 100, 4914 AG, Breda

JAPAN, Kazumasa Matsumoto (2CV Club BAC), 21-10 Sugamo 4 Chome, T 170 Tosima-Ku, Tokyo

LUXEMBOURG, Nico Berrend, Rue De Samatorium 29, L-9425, Vianden

NORWAY, Oluf Berrum, Kristian 1V'S Gt. 12, N-Oslo

SWEDEN, Per Westin (Svenska Citroën Klub), Virebergsvagen 11, S-171 40 Solna

USA, Richard Bonfond, 1103 S. Stelling Road, Cupertino, California 95014

YUGOSLAVIA, Peter Pogorevc, Ribnisko Selo 3, Kocevarjeva 17, 62000 Maribor

GREAT BRITAIN, R.A. MacQueen, 14 Northcote Street, Leamington Spa, Warwickshire

Left: Last minute beauty treatment before 1982 Waggel. *(J. McNamara)*

Below: The Swiss showing a natural flair for precision parking beneath their flag. *(J. McNamara)*

Left: German cabriolet. (J. McNamara)

Below: What to do when the front rusts on an Ami. (J. McNamara)

APPENDIX I

A BRIEF GUIDE TO MODEL NOMENCLATURE FOR POST WAR 2CVs

MODEL

A First presented at the 1948 Paris *Salon*. 375cc engine, magneto ignition, rope pull starter, 6 volt electrics, one rear and one stop light. Max speed 65kph, consumption 4-5 litres per 100Ks. Coachwork finished in metallic grey with grey upholstery. 125 x 400 tyres. Put on sale in July 1949 at 235,000 Francs with 9.5bhp chassis nos 1-924. 1950, car as above chassis nos 925 to 7,100 price 340,000 Francs.

AU 250Kg capacity *cammionette* with pretty, flattened, oval rear windows went on sale in 1951. Key ignition and door locks became available in 1952 chassis nos 7101-21850 (1951), 21851-43,150 (1952). 1953, March oval surround dropped from grille mounted chevrons, cream wheels became available. July, four bladed fan replaced the previous eight bladed article. Chassis nos 43,151-77,950.

AZ Introduced September 1954 with 425cc engine and centrifugal clutch with six bladed fan. Jan to April experimental relocation of side mounted suspension. First appearance of window retaining catches on French built cars. In November compression was raised from 6.2 to 7; max speed given as 70kph, consumption 5 litres per 100Ks. Chassis nos 77,951 to 121,200.

AZU *Cammionnette* variant of the above, introduced concurrently.

AZL Introduced December 1956 this was a deluxe version offering a choice of colours, enlarged rear window, flashing indicators as standard fitting and choice of trim colours.

AZL3 Introduced in Belgium featured six light coachwork.

AZUL Again introduced in Belgium in 1956 known as the *Weekend* it was a station wagon version of the AZUL.

AZLP On sale in 1957 featured metal boot lid and symmetrical rear number plate mounting.

AW *Sahara* introduced March 1958. 2 x 425cc engines rated at 12bhp each driving through centrifugal clutches. Choice of 155 x 400, or 155 x 380 tyres. Max quoted speed 100khp. Consumption on one engine 5-6 litres per 100Ks, on both 9 litres per 100Ks on road, 11 to 12 off road.

AMI6 Based on chassis of 2CV with 602cc variation of original engine.

AZC Introduced in March '62. The C denoted *Commerciale*. Features included folding rear seat, underbonnet mounting for spare wheel and a rather primitive type of hatch back.

AZAM Arrived in March 1963 introducing twin rear stop lights as standard fitting on French built cars. Chrome overriders and wheel trims.

AZAM6 Featured the *Ami6* 602cc engine and originated from the Belgian factory again introduced in March '63.

AK350 Introduced in April '63 this was basically the AZU with side lights, square and enlarged rear windows, an improved payload (350Kg), corrugations removed from the tonneau and a lengthened rear load area. The 602cc engine was utilised.

AMI6 Brake, this was an estate version of the *Ami6* introduced 1963.

Dyane Introduced August 1967. Known as *Dyane* 4 featuring 425cc engine. This was changed almost immediately to the later 435cc unit and the *Dyane* 6 was introduced concurrently with this change.

MEHARI Introduced in May 1968. First French vehicle of ABS plastic construction to achieve series production. Mechanically similar to AZAM6.

AMI8 Arrived on the scene in 1969 at the Geneva Show with 35bhp version of the 602cc engine. Disc brakes were standardised and later made the transition to the rest of the range.

2CV4 & 2CV6 Introduced in February 1970. 2CV4 with 435cc 25bhp engine and the 2CV6 with 602cc 33bhp engine.

AK400 Introduced in July 1970 with a high top option and carrying capacity increased to 475Kg. 2CV6 engine.

AK250 Introduced in January 1972 based on the old AZU but with square corrugations and the 435cc engine.

2CV Special A back to basics exercise orginally only for the home market. Featuring the 435cc engine in four light coachwork. This was subsequently changed to the 602cc power plant in 1970.

ACADIANE The replacement for the AK400 and 250 introduced in March 1978 with *Dyane* style coachwork and 602cc 31bhp engine. All are Spanish built.

FAF 1978. See cross country Citroëns.

APPENDIX II

BUYING A USED 2CV
Some of the pitfalls

1) Brakes. Check the brakes firstly by taking the hands from the steering wheel whilst in motion and applying foot brake; if brakes pull to either side something is obviously amiss. Repeat the test with the handbrake. When car is stationary apply a good hard pressure on the brake pedal. If it gradually sinks after a few seconds discontinue negotiations.

2) To check for undue wear in wheel bearings and kingpins jack up the front of the vehicle take hold of the top and bottom of front wheels and check for play. Whilst car is jacked up get a friend to hold the steering wheel and try to move the wheels. Any movement here is likely to be expensive.

3) On early models fitted with six volt electrics check that everything is functioning and examine condition of wiring.

4) If steering is unduly heavy swivels may be seized while if the steering wheel rises and drops when turned it could spell trouble with the pinion bearing.

5) Examine the tyres for any excessive scuffing from bad tracking.

6) If the synchos are worn the chances are that third gear will be snagging.

7) Although noisy tappets are acceptable any other knocks from beneath the bonnet should be avoided like the plague.

8) Corrosion spots. Floor by the drivers feet and the bottom of the door pillars. Inside edges of sills. Chassis at rear axle mountings. Rear bump stop mountings in boot. On vans check valence beneath rear door, spare wheel and petrol tank covers. With *Dyanes*, check upper tailgate and bottom of doors. The *Ami* can rust almost anywhere and frequently does.

9) Avoid cracked or crazed bodywork on *Meharis*.

Note: Groans or oinks from the suspension need not cause too great distress as an application of vegetable based oil to the side mounted spring cylinders will usually cure this.

APPENDIX III

Excerpts from the technical report written by Ken Garrett, CEng, FIMechE, MRAeS, which formed the basis for two articles on the now defunct **Automobile Engineer** *in March and May 1954. A full copy of this report is available from Great Ouse Press for £1.00 to cover handling and postage.*

I. Technical Review of the Engine

Specification

ENGINE: *Two cylinders, horizontally opposed. Bore and stroke 62mm × 62mm. Swept volume 375cm³. Four-stroke. Maximum b.h.p. 9 at 3,500 r.p.m. Maximum b.m.e.p. and torque respectively 110 lb/in² and 16.6 lb-ft, at 1,800 r.p.m. Compression ratio 6.2:1. Two-bearing, two-throw crankshaft, built up from five pieces. Push rod operated, overhead valves. Solex carburettor and Guiot fuel lift pump. Fuel tank capacity 4.4 gallons.*

Interest in the Citroën 2CV has been intensified in this country by the announcement that it is to be assembled at the Citroën factory at Slough. Despite the fact that this is one of the most unconventional cars produced in large quantities since the war, it is also one of the most successful in its country of origin. Its success is in part due to the compact engine design, which has made possible the adoption of a front-wheel-drive arrangement. This not only allows exceptionally easy access to the whole of the engine and transmission system, but also leaves the maximum amount of space free in the body.

As a result, the cost and overall dimensions of the vehicle have been kept to a minimum. However, the economies effected by the use of the front-wheel-drive layout are to some extent offset by the fact that one additional sliding joint, two extra universal joints and an extra pair of rolling element bearings are required, as compared with the more conventional rear drive arrangement.

Another attractive feature of this vehicle is its low fuel consumption in terms of miles per gallon. This has been obtained by employing an engine of small capacity, 375 cm³, and by keeping the weight of the vehicle to a minimum. The power output of the unit is 9 b.h.p., which represents 24 b.h.p./litre, and is low even for a car of such a small size. From the figure of 1,100 lb, for the kerb weight, given in the specification panel, it can be seen that the power:weight ratio is 18.35 b.h.p./ton.

Other details of this engine are given in the accompanying specification panel. The maximum b.m.e.p. and torque are 110 lb/in² and 16 lb-ft respectively, and are developed at 1,800 r.p.m. A bore:stroke ratio of 1:1 has been adopted and the connecting rod length:stroke ratio is approximately 1.93:1. At the engine speed at which maximum b.h.p. is developed, the mean piston speed is 1,430 ft/min. This speed is very low and although, as has already been stated, it is not the only factor that influences cylinder wear, it undoubtedly tends to prolong the periods between rebores. The output per square inch piston area is 0.95 b.h.p.

An integral crankcase and sump is employed. It is an aluminium alloy casting divided in a vertical, longitudinal plane, and the halves are dowel located. At the rear, four 10 mm diameter studs are carried to secure the transmission casing to the crankcase. Two housings are cored in the front end of the crankcase. The inner one, the base of which is open to the sump, completely encloses the driving gear on the crankshaft extension and the half-speed wheel. Behind the driving gear is the front bearing of the crankshaft and in front of it is a ring pressed on to the shaft. This ring has an oil return scroll machined on its periphery; it is housed in a bore in the front wall of the crankcase.

In front of this is the dynamo, the hub of which is on a taper on the end of the crankshaft. A forward extension of the hub carries the blower rotor, and is internally tapered to receive a tapered plug pulled into it by a bolt screwed into the front end of the crankshaft. Dogs for the starter handle are formed on the plug. The shell of the dynamo, in which the field coils are mounted, is bolted to the crankcase. With this arrangement, there are no bearings in the dynamo and therefore reliability may be improved and cost reduced. However, the unit has to be designed specifically for the engine and this tends to offset the advantage of cost reduction. Moreover, in some engine designs, because of crankshaft deflections, the adoption of such a layout might present some difficulties.

Crankshaft, connecting rods and pistons

The crankshaft and connecting rods, together with the front journal bearing and the pressed-on helical gear and oil return scroll ring at the front end, are fitted to the engine as a complete assembly during manufacture, and the components cannot be obtained separately as service spares. This is because the crankshaft is built up from five pieces, and the connecting rods, together with the big end bearing bushes, are assembled on to the crank pins before they are pressed into the webs. The five pieces are: the front and rear ends complete with webs, the two crank pins, the end of which are shouldered to locate them axially in the webs, and the oval centre web. In an engine of much higher power rating, the press fit alone would hardly be adequate to resist the torque loading of the shaft, but apparently movement of the components relative to one another is not experienced in this application.

This method of manufacturing crankshafts may well solve more problems than it creates.

Aluminium alloy pistons with domed crowns are used. They are somewhat unusual in that at the thrust faces, the base of the skirt of each piston is extended downwards. This presumably is to increase the bearing area available to take the thrust. It may also be intended to improve piston cooling. However, many authorities consider that by far the greatest proportion of the heat flow to the cylinder walls takes place through the rings and not between the contacting faces of the piston and the bore.

The pistons are of such a sturdy design that they appear to be capable of dissipating much greater heat flow than is likely to be experienced in an engine of such low rating. However, the precautions taken in this respect may well be justified in view of the fact that in a motor car powered by an air-cooled engine, the flow of air over the cylinders is not so great as in, for instance, a motor cycle. Three compression rings, each with a face width of 2 mm, and one oil control ring, with a face width of 3.5 mm, are fitted to each piston.

Timing gear, camshaft and valve gear

An unusual feature of this engine is that, so far as spares are concerned, the camshaft, its front bearing, the half speed wheel, the mechanical advance and retard mechanism and the contact breaker cam are supplied as a complete assembly. The contact breaker cam and automatic advance and retard mechanism are mounted on a forward extension of the camshaft. Behind these is machined an oil return scroll that works in a bore in the front wall of the crankcase. Immediately to the rear of this is the eccentric on which bears the push rod that actuates the fuel pump mounted on a boss on the right-hand side of the crankcase

At the front of the camshaft, a bush-type bearing is employed. It is located between the half speed wheel and a flange on the rear end of the journal. Axial location of the whole assembly is effected by a stepped dowel, the small diameter portion of which registers in a hole in the bearing, and the larger end is in the housing. The rear end of the camshaft bears directly in the oil pump body, and the eccentric gear of the pump is keyed on to a rearward extension of the shaft.

The tappets are 24 mm diameter by 51 mm long and are of unusual design. They are of tubular construction and have hardened pads in their ends. Hardened spherical end fittings are carried at both ends of each of the push rods, which are 220 mm long. The rods are housed in tubes, the outer peripheries of which are shouldered at each end. The outer end of each tube is pressed and spigoted into the cylinder head, and then fixed by peening. Over the inner end is passed a washer, which is located against the shoulder on the tube and retains a coil spring. The inner end of this spring bears on an assembly, comprising a sealing ring and cupped retainer washer, round the end of the tube and presses it against the end face of the tappet housing bored in the crankcase.

The outer end of each push rod seats in the cupped end of a tappet adjusting screw on one end of the rocker arm. This arm is centrally pivoted and on its other end a cone is formed with its apex pointing inwards towards the head. The cone seats in a hole in a retainer washer for a light, coil-type return spring, which has the function of ensuring that the rocker at all times remains seated on the end of the push rod. On the other end of the boss of the rocker is another arm, extended in the same direction as the one with the cone end; it has a hardened end pad that bears on the valve in the usual manner.

There are two rocker shafts per cylinder. They are 12 mm diameter by 100 mm long. Their axes are vertical and they are carried between the two valves, which are set at an included angle of 70 deg in a horizontal plane. The pedestals that support the rocker shafts are cast integrally with the aluminium alloy head, and the upper pair form bosses through which two of the three cylinder holding down studs are passed. This arrangement is a good one from the point of view of accessibility to the holding down nuts.

Single springs are employed on the valves. Each has a free length of 38 mm and, under a load of 31-40 kg, its length is 24 mm, while under a load of 18-20 kg, it is 31 mm long. In the exhaust valve assembly, the lower end of the spring bears on a shroud which fits over the end of the valve guide to prevent it from being over-oiled, but in the inlet assembly the spring seats on a plain washer round in the end of the guide. Each spring is retained by a shouldered washer, in which a hole is drilled eccentrically. A slot is cut in the centre of the washer to break out into the hole, and two flats are machined near the end of the valve stem. After the stem has been passed into the eccentric hole, it is slid into the slot in which it is retained by the end of the stem dropping into a counterbore in the centre of the washer.

The face width of both valve seats is 0l9-1.5 mm. In the inlet ports, the included angle of the seats is 120 deg, and the face width is limited by cutting back the bore of the seat at an included angle of 26 deg. A 60 deg cut is effected in the bores of the exhaust valve seats to limit the width of the face, the included angle of which is 90 deg. The tappet clearances are 0.15 mm inlet and 0.20 mm exhaust.

Cylinder heads and barrels

Three cylinder-holding-down studs are employed and they are waisted to 8 mm diameter between the ends. They pass through the cylinder heads and are screwed into the crankcase. To prevent seepage of oil down the studs, cap nuts are used to hold down the cylinder head and barrel assembly. A single, 7 mm diameter stud is screwed into the centre of the cylinder head and a cap nut on it holds down the rocker cover. A joint washer is fitted between the head and the cover to prevent loss of oil. If this washer is not in good condition, or is badly fitted so that it leaks, it is possible in time to lose all the lubricating oil from the engine. It is difficult, however, to imagine such a large amount of lubricant being lost without its being noticed in time to prevent serious damage.

A spherical combustion chamber is incorporated in the head, and it has been necessary to machine a small recess in the crown of the piston to provide clearance for the inner edge of each valve during the overlap

Both the inlet and exhaust manifolds are fabricated from steel tube and sheet metal. The inlet pipes from each side pass over the engine and are welded to the riser pipe at the centre. This junction is enclosed in a heater jacket, also fabricated from sheet steel, through which is passed the exhaust gas from the right-hand cylinder. On earlier models, a metal screen was interposed between this jacket and the carburettor mounted above it, but it is no longer provided, since it has been found unnecessary. The Solex carburettor is held down by two 7 mm diameter studs; a 6 mm thick, insulating washer is interposed between it and the riser pipe. A simple felt-element-type air cleaner is fitted on top of the carburettor.

A shouldered rubber sleeve connects a pipe from the air cleaner to a branch pipe on the oil filler tube assembly bolted on top of the crankcase. In the end of the branch pipe is a simple disc-type non-return valve to ensure that air can only pass out of the crankcase. This is an important feature because there is no oil filter in the lubrication system.

Exhaust system

The exhaust from the right-hand cylinder is carried through a pipe, over the top of the engine to the heater box, which is round the junction between the induction pipes and the riser. It then passes out through another pipe to the left-hand side, where it is joined by a branch from the other cylinder. The manifold pipe terminates a short distance in front of this junction. A spherical seating ring is welded on its end, and the belled end of the exhaust pipe is clamped to it by means of a diametrically split ring, of channel section. Two 7 mm diameter bolts hold together the halves of the ring. The exhaust pipe is carried forwards and then downwards and to the rear, to an expansion box under the left-hand cylinder. From this box, another pipe carries the exhaust into the silencer which is mounted transversely beneath the gearbox.

Lubrication system

Oil is drawn through a strainer in the base of the sump into a long, thimble fitting on which the strainer is mounted and thence through a radial hole in the fitting into a vertical passage drilled in the rear wall of the sump and crankcase casting. From this passage, it passes into the eccentric-gear type oil pump. The eccentric gear is keyed on to the rear end of the camshaft. It drives an internally toothed annulus which is free to rotate in the housing, and which meshes at the top of the gear. Below, a crescent-section separator vane fills the clearance between the tips of the teeth of the gear and the annulus. There are thirteen teeth on the gear and sixteen on the annulus.

The oil outlet channel is cored in the cover plate and directs the lubricant into the hollow camshaft. Radial holes in the front end of the camshaft pass the oil into a large section annular groove round its front journal. From this groove, the lubricant passes into a drilled passage in the end of which is a spring-loaded ball-type relief valve housed in the side of the crankcase.

II. The Chassis

Specification

TRANSMISSION: *Single dry plate clutch, 160 mm diameter (6.3 in). Overall gear ratios: top 5.7:1, third 7.5:1, second 12.55:1, first 25.9:1, reverse 28.1:1.*

FINAL DRIVE: *Spiral bevel, with a ratio of 3.87:1. Needle roller universal jointed shafts to the front wheels.*

SUSPENSION: *Single leading arms on each side at the front and trailing arms at the rear. Coil type, compression springs are incorporated in an interconnecting link between the front and rear arms on each side.*

SHOCK ABSORBERS: *A dynamic absorber of Citroën design mounted on each wheel hub.*

STEERING: *Rack and pinion. $2\frac{1}{4}$ turns from lock to lock. Turning circle 35 ft 6 in to the left and 35 ft 3 in to the right.*

BRAKES: *Lockheed hydraulic leading and trailing shoe brakes at front and rear. Drum diameters: front 7.8 in, rear 7.87 in. Shoe width 1.55 in. Shoe area: front 34.1 in^2, rear 30.8 in^2.*

TYRES: *Michelin 125 × 400 mm. Pressure: front 14.25 lb/in^2, rear 15.75 lb/in^2. Disc type wheel, secured to the hub by three bolts.*

DIMENSIONS: *Wheelbase 7 ft $9\frac{5}{16}$ in, unladen. Track, front and rear 4 ft $1\frac{5}{8}$ in. Ground clearance $7\frac{1}{2}$ in. Overall dimensions: length 12 ft $4\frac{3}{4}$ in, width 4 ft $10\frac{3}{16}$ in, height 5 ft 3 in. Kerb weight 1.100 lb. Unladen weight distribution: front 58.8 per cent, rear 41.2 per cent.*

The power:weight ratio of the Citroën 2CV is low. In fact the figure as calculated from the kerb weight of the car is 18.35 b.h.p./ton. As a result of this low ratio, the acceleration is poor and maximum speed is only approximately 40 m.p.h. The overall fuel consumption, however, is approximately 63-64 m.p.g. These comments on the performance are not intended to be taken as adverse criticism, for it must be borne in mind that this vehicle was designed as an economy car. In this respect, the car has been a great success in France where it probably has no equal in its class.

The design is noteworthy for a number of original features and for the ingenuity displayed in solving the design problems, many of which are peculiar to this type of vehicle. For instance, both the head lamps are mounted on a horizontal tube which can be rotated by means of a control rod to adjust the angle of elevation of the beam from inside the car. This is necessary because the suspension layout is such that the attitude of the vehicle varies appreciably with the load. The horn button and lamp and dip switches are in a single unit on the steering column, and an ammeter is installed on the instrument panel. Although the windscreen wipers are powered by the speedometer drive, they can also be manually operated. A dip stick is employed instead of a petrol gauge.

In general, the body panels are of simple form so that wear of the press tools is reduced to a minimum. Moreover, since most of the panels are relatively flat, repair to damage done during service should be easy. As can be seen in the accompanying illustration showing the seating arrangement, a tubular framework is used to support the panels. There has been no attempt to conceal spot welding where to have done so would have increased production costs.

The seats are exceptionally comfortable for this class of car. They might be described as a cross between the bench and bucket types. The two front seats are formed by a single tubular structure based on three vertical longitudinal frames, one on each side and another midway between them. These three support the seat and squab frames, which carry rubber strips, in tension, with a canvas overlay. The rubber deflects to conform to the shape of the body and thereby gives a degree of support similar to that afforded by a bucket type seat.

Clutch

The clutch is unusual in that instead of being housed in a dished pressed-steel casing, it is in the cupped flywheel, the rear of which is closed by a steel plate secured by ten 6 mm diameter set bolts. A fairly conventional centre plate, faced on each side with a 160 mm diameter friction lining, is employed. The centre of the plate is dished to the rear and riveted to a splined hub carried on a shaft overhung from the final drive unit.

Six pressure springs are employed. Their free length is 33.7 mm, and under a load of 25-27 kg the length is 25 mm. These springs are housed in flanged thimbles in holes in the rear cover, and bear against the presser plate. The rear cover and presser plate assembly is held together by three special bolts with round heads counter-sunk in the front face of the plate, and the threaded ends of the bolts are passed through holes in the ends of the three withdrawal levers. A coil spring is fitted round the shank of each bolt between the rear face of the presser plate and the withdrawal lever. The hole in the end of each withdrawal lever has two small slots diametrically opposed on each side of its periphery. Two projections on the nut that holds the assembly together register in these slots and the end of the bolt shank has a screwdriver slot cut in it, so that adjustment to compensate for wear of the thrust ring is easily effected.

Gearbox

As is usual with front wheel drive arrangements, the final-drive unit is between the engine and the gearbox. The drive is transmitted to the mainshaft by a long primary shaft, and the crown wheel of the spiral bevel, final drive unit is integral with the layshaft. Thus, all gears are indirect. The ratios are: top 1.474:1, third 1.94:1, second 3.24:1, first 6.69:1, and reverse 7.26:1. All four forward speeds are engaged through synchro units and helical gears are employed for all except the first and reverse trains.

A common casing is employed for the final drive and gearbox, so the same lubricating oil is used for both. Mobiloil GX is recommended, and the capacity is 2.2 pints. The casing is in three pieces. The main part of the box is divided vertically in the plane containing the axes of the final drive shafts. Integral with the front portion is the bellhousing, which does not totally enclose the flywheel, but extends above and below it and is in effect a large bracket by means of which the transmission unit is attached to the engine. This leaves part of the flywheel and ring gear exposed so that, when the engine is running, care must be taken to avoid getting clothing, etc., caught by the rotating parts.

Final drive

A final-drive unit of simple design is employed; it is housed in a casing that is divided in the transverse, vertical plane in which are the axes of the fixed portions of the half shafts. The swinging portions of the half shafts are inclined rearwards so that the suspension cross-tube can pass behind the gearbox. A final drive ratio of 8:31 has been adopted.

Swivel pin assembly and steering system

The 17 mm diameter swivel pin is carried in two knuckles on an extension of the forging that forms the housing for the wheel hub and driving shaft assembly. The lower bearing bush is 17.062 mm inside diameter by 21 mm outside diameter by 33 mm long, and the upper bush is of the same dimensions except that its length is 19 mm. Both are of phosphor bronze. They are spaced approximately 64 mm apart, as measured between the adjacent ends of the bushes.

The steering arrangement is a conventional rack-and-pinion layout with a three-piece track rod. However, the centre member, which is formed by a short length of the rack, is so small that the geometry is virtually the same as that of a two-piece track rod system. At the outer end of each of the two rods is the ball-and-socket joint mentioned in the previous paragraph. An eye in the inner end of each rod carries a ball fitting for another ball-and-socket joint. The ball is on a stem tapered and keyed into the eye and retained by a slotted nut, and two diametrically opposed flats are machined on it, so that it can be passed through a relatively small slot in the front face of the socket. The socket is a tube spun over a head up-ended on the rack, and is self-adjusting for wear.

Assembled into the end of the tube, in the following order, are: a distance tube that separates the end of the rack from one half of the left-hand spherical bearing, which is placed in position next, then the ball fitting is inserted through the slot in the front of the tube. Next, the other half of the socket bearing is asembled into the tube, followed by a compression spring inside a distance tube, and then half of the right-hand spherical bearing. The ball fitting on this side is inserted through another slot in the tube, and finally, the other half of the bearing is inserted, and a cupped end-cap is screwed in and locked by a split pin.

The rack-and-pinion assembly is housed in the cross-tube that carries the pivots of the suspension arms. Bolted inside the front of this tube is a pressed steel housing for the ball and socket end of the rack. A spherical bearing-ring is riveted round the socket tube to reduce the friction between it and the pressed steel housing. During assembly, the rack is passed through a slot in the front face of the cross-tube. This slot also provides the necessary clearance for the ball fittings to move from side-to-side with the rack. It is closed by a plate that is mounted on and moves with the ball fittings. This plate is spring loaded against the cross-tube. The other end of the rack is, of course, carried in the pinion housing which is welded inside the cross-tube.

A spring-loaded plunger underneath the rack forces it into engagement with the pinion, which has seven teeth of helical form. This plunger is retained in its housing by a cupped plug that is screwed in and locked by a split pin.

Suspension

The suspension system comprises four bell-crank levers mounted one on each end of two tubular cross members bolted on top of the frame. Each lever has two arms, one long and one short. The long ones on the front pair extend forwards and those on the rear pair extend backwards to carry the wheels. All four short arms extend downwards and each makes an angle with the long one of appreciably more than 90 deg. The two short members on each side are interconnected, and the main suspension coil springs are incorporated in the interconnecting links. Thus, when the front wheels ride over a bump, the motion is transmitted through the bell cranks and links to raise the rear end and so reduce pitching. Unequal weight distribution between the front and rear of the vehicle tends to make it settle down at one end. To counter this, that is, to centralize the system, an additional pair of springs is fitted on each side, where they are mounted on the ends of the housings for the main suspension springs.

On each side of the vehicle is the assembly comprising two centralizing springs and two coil-type suspension springs in a large diameter tubular housing. The centralizing springs are of the conical volute-type and they are carried in the outwardly cupped end plates of the housing. All the springs are in compression. The free length of the front coil spring is 195 mm and that of the rear one is 170 mm. When fitted, their overall length, together with the spring retainers between them, is 417 mm. Both springs have an overall diameter of 100 mm; the wire gauge of the front one is 14.4 mm and that of the rear is 15.2 mm. The front springs have eight coils, and the rear ones seven. At the front, the volute-type spring has a free length of 64 mm and the length of that at the rear is 38 mm.

On each side of the vehicle, the tie rods interconnecting the front and rear bell cranks are passed through holes in the centre of the end plates of the cylinder, and their inner ends are secured to piston-type retainers which seat on the inner ends of the main suspension coil springs. The outer ends of these two coil springs bear against the end plates of the housing, and the apex of each centralizing spring bears against a shoulder on a tube mounted on a bracket on the frame side member. This tube extends through the hole in the end plate to locate the whole assembly radially.

This arrangement appears effectively to counter any tendency to pitch. Friction dampers at the pivots of the bell cranks further assist in reducing pitching, but it would appear that the primary function of these dampers is to reduce the amplitudes of the lower frequency vertical oscillations of the sprung mass. Resonant vibrations of the sprung mass are further discouraged by the variable rate obtained with the bell crank geometry.

The tubular arms of the suspension units are each welded to a sleeve that forms the housings for the pivot bearings. The seal at the outer end is round the ring nut, while that at the inner end bears on the collar on the cross tube.

Wheel hop is countered effectively by dynamic absorbers mounted vertically one on each wheel hub. Each of these absorbers is in a sealed tubular housing, about $11\frac{1}{4}$ in long by $3\frac{1}{8}$ in outside diameter. A false base is pressed on the lower end of the housing to protect it against damage when passing over exceptionally rough terrain. Inside the unit, a simple mass-spring system is installed. The lower end of the spring is carried in a ring, the inner periphery of which is grooved to receive it. A flange round the outer periphery of this ring is clamped between the bottom of the tubular housing and its end cap.

It seems that damping is afforded by the passage of air, as it is displaced from one side of the mass to the other, along the clearance between the hole in the mass and the tube. A small quantity of oil is carried in the base of the unit so that air pressure during the downward stroke of the mass forces the oil in through the lower hole, up the tube and out of the top hole, from which it is sprayed on to the conical end of the mass, and runs on to the walls of the housing for lubrication purposes.

However, the system certainly works very well in practice. When driven over extremely rough terrain, the vehicle bounces to an extent which is somewhat frightening to anyone accustomed to more conventional systems. This bounce is, of course, at the fairly low natural frequency of the sprung mass on the suspension. The vehicle also rolls when cornering. Despite these characteristics, the Citroën 2CV is perfectly safe, and the rolling and bouncing behaviour probably tends to discourage abusive handling of such a small car. An outstanding feature of the suspension system unit is the almost complete absence of wheel hop.

Rear wheels, brakes and frame

The stub axle for each rear wheel is welded in its suspension arm, and the pressed steel brake back plate is welded on to it. Outboard of the back plate, the axle is shouldered for the two-row ball bearing that carries the wheel hub. This bearing has a single outer race and a two-piece inner race. The inner race is pulled on by a nut on the end of the stub axle, and the outer race is retained in its housing by a ring nut screwed into the outer end of the hub. A domed cap pressed into the ring nut retains the grease and prevents the ingress of foreign matter. A lip-type oil seal is housed in the inner end of the hub, and bears on the stub axle. The wheel is secured by three nuts and studs to a flange round the hub. These studs, which have round heads up-ended at their inner ends, serve to secure the brake drum to the inner face of the flange. This arrangement is unusual in that the drum is not spigoted on to the flange.

Lockheed hydraulic, leading and trailing shoe brakes are fitted both at the front and at the rear. The drum diameter is 8.87 in and the shoe width is 1.55 in. At the front, the shoe area is 31.4 in^2 and at the rear it is 30.8 in^2. A brake pedal travel of 3.55 in has been allowed. The handbrake control is of the pistol-grip type and it actuates the front brakes. This allows a short length of cable to be used, which is an advantage both economically and in that it tends to make the control more positive in action. The reason it is practicable in this vehicle is, of course, that the brakes are mounted on the final drive casing and therefore do not move with the wheels when they are steered.

The frame is of exceptionally rigid design and its overall length is 3,540 mm (11 ft 7$\frac{1}{2}$ in). Rigidity is of far more importance to the quality of ride than is generally realized. A flexible frame tends to give the occupants of the vehicle a subconcious sense of insecurity when the vehicle traverses anything but smooth ground. The vague uneasiness experienced is interpreted by the conscious mind into a feeling that the whole structure is unstable, and that the ride is not all it might be.

Over the whole length of the chassis, the side members of the frame are straight. They are of box section, formed by two channel sections with their flanges extended outwards. One is shallow and is placed inside the other which is of deeper section. The flanges of the shallow one are turned outwards through 180 deg and are wrapped round the flanges of the deeper one to which they are spot welded. This strengthens the flange enough to carry the suspension cross tubes. Over the centre portion of the frame, the inner channel at each side is cranked inwards to form a kind of cruciform bracing over the length between the front and rear suspension cross-tubes. The centre parallel portions of the cranked members on each side are approximately 8 in apart and are parallel for a distance of about 2 ft 11 in.

Between points immediately in front of the front suspension cross-tube and behind the rear one, the whole of the frame is completely boxed in by closing plates welded on top of, and below, the side members of the cruciform members. Spot welding is employed for the junction of the plate to the cruciform members, and at the outer edges of the plate where it is carried in the 180 deg bend of the flange of the shallow channel to which it is spot welded. An indication of the width of the frame can be gained from the fact that the distance between the pairs of bolt holes drilled in the flanges of the side members for mounting the suspension cross tubes is 556 mm, or about 22 in.

At the rear, the ends of the top and bottom plates are cut back towards the centre in a semi-circular fashion between the side members, and the end is closed by a channel section, the flanges of which extend rearwards and are spot welded to the plates. A similar arrangement is employed at the front, but the lower plate is extended forwards under the cross member beneath the gearbox. This cross member is of top hat section, and its flanges are welded to the extension of the bottom plate. Its top face is extended on each side to overlap the frame side members to which it is welded. Between this cross member and the semi-circular channel that closes the front end of the centre portion of the frame, louvres are punched in the bottom plate for drainage purposes.

At the forward end of the frame, there is another box section cross member formed by a top hat section with a closing plate welded to its flanges, which are at the front. The top and bottom walls of this section are extended on each side to overlap the side members, to which they are welded. There are no cross members at the rear of the frame, but two tubular ones in the boxed-in portion between the suspension cross-tubes are passed through the side members and the cruciform member. They are spaced with their axes 597 mm (23½ in) apart, and they overhang each side of the frame far enough to carry the suspension spring assembly. Top hat section outrigger extensions are welded on top of them to carry the body. The outer ends of these outriggers on each side are spaced apart by another top hat section welded on. This forms the body sill and supports the front seat.

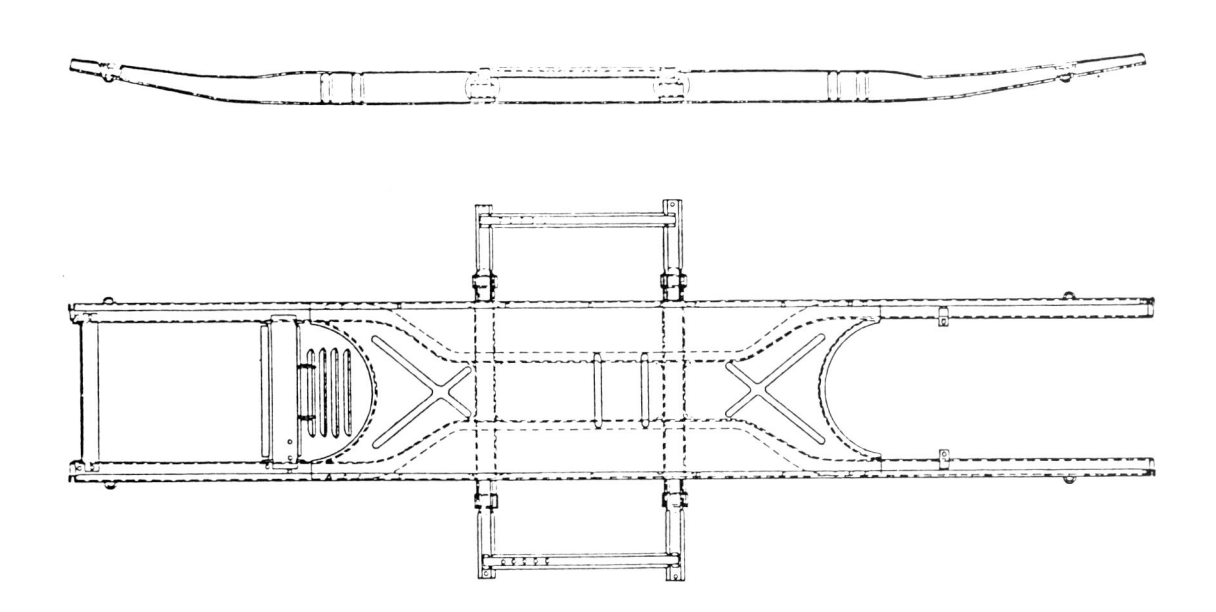

As can be seen the chassis is formed by extremely light but exceptionally stiff members allowing minimal body weight.

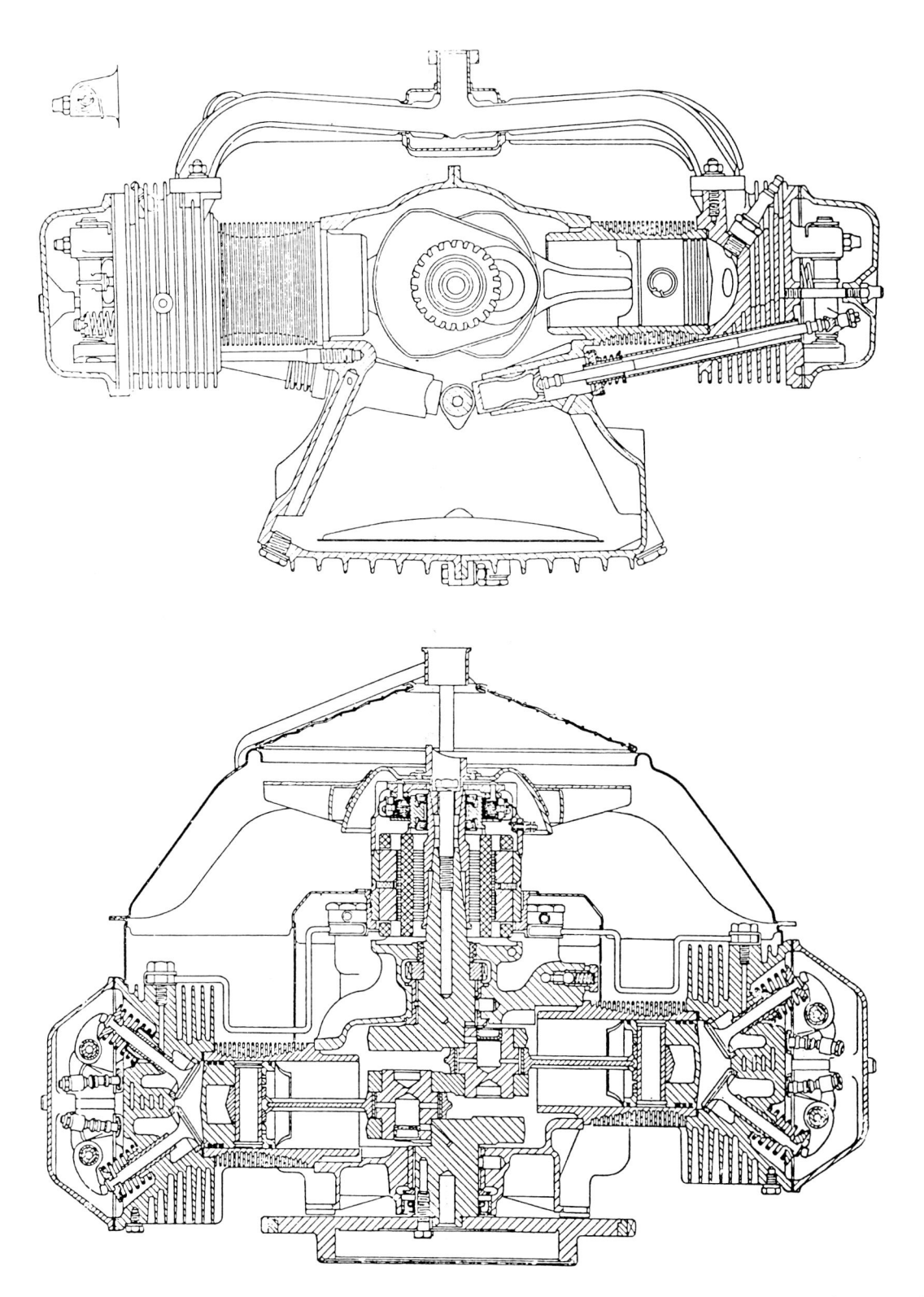

Cut away showing the internal configuration of the 375cc, 62 x 62 mm engine.

Exploded view of cylinder/crankcase assembly clearly showing oil cooler.

APPENDIX IV

SOME CITROËN LITERATURE

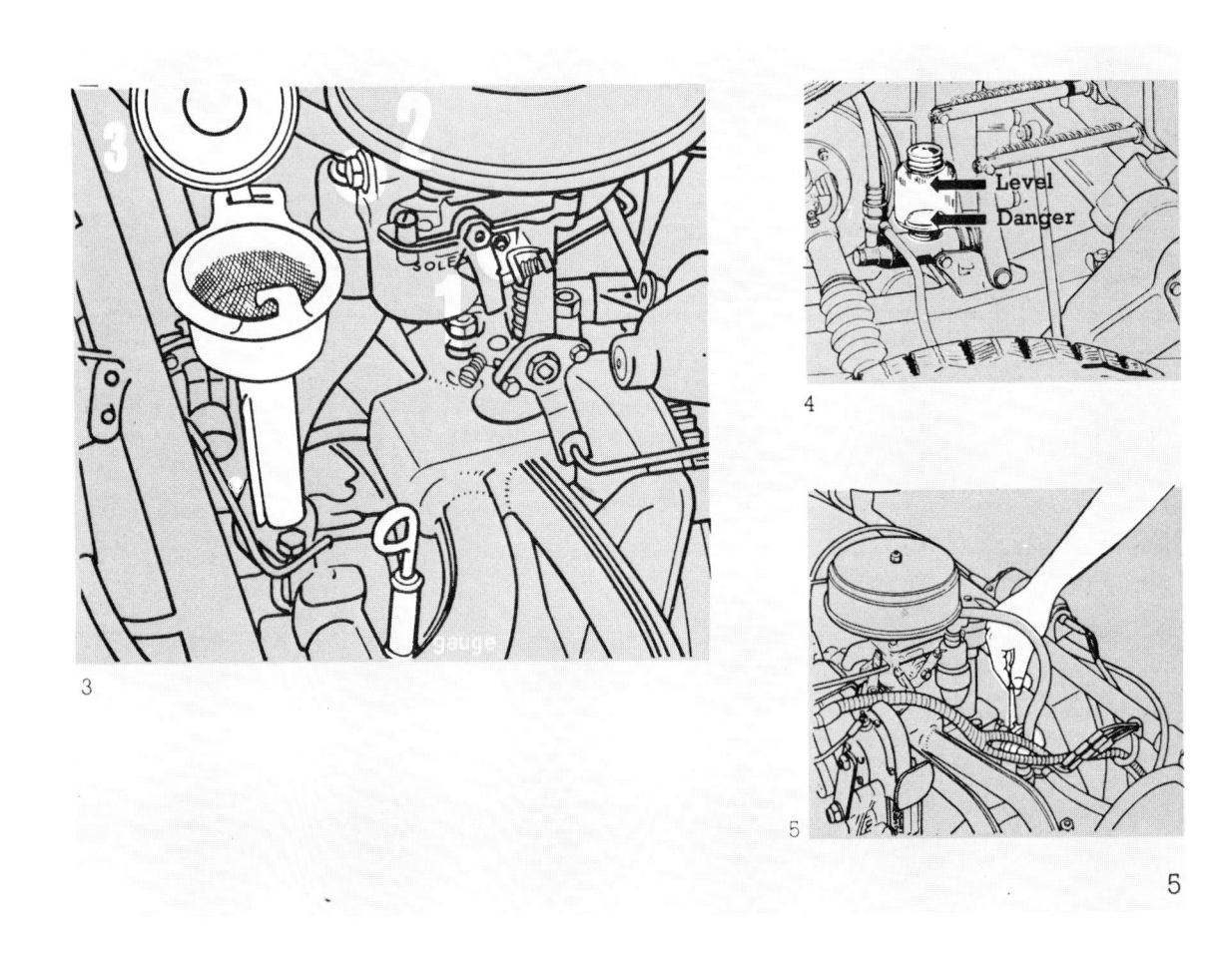

illustrations from original British handbook.

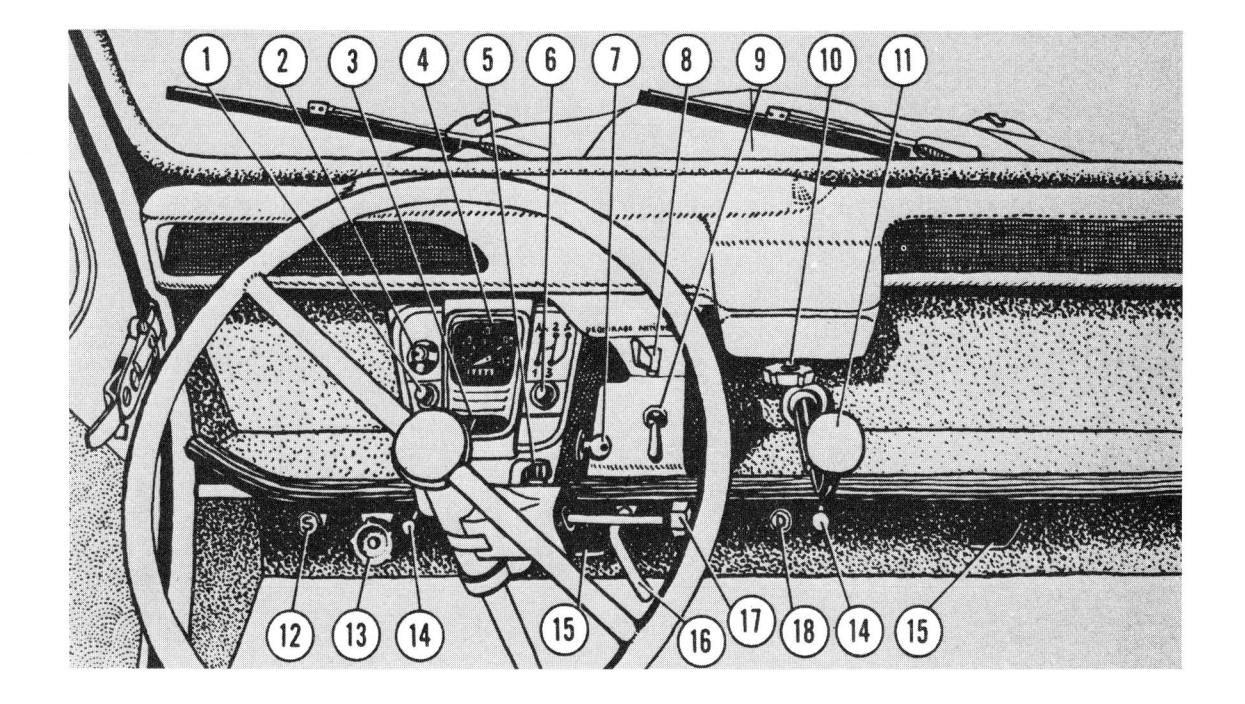

Dashboard (figure 6).

1. Parking lights.
2. Generator signal light:
   This signal lights up when the engine is idling, but must go out at normal operating speed. If it remains lit, have the electrical system checked as soon as possible by a CITROËN dealer. With the engine stopped, its bright signal will remind yon that the ignition switch has not been turned off.
3. Essence gauge.
4. Speedometer.
5. Heat or defrosting control switch.
6. Windshield wiper.
   To start it, pull out the knob.
7. Ignition switch.
8. Defrosting control.
9. Direction indicators:
   They work for about ten seconds and then automatically stop You can interrupt their action by turning the switch in the opposite direction by hand.
10. Ventilation control.
11. Gear shift lever.
12. Choke.
13. Headlight control.
14. Heat control.
15. Heat or defrosting control switch.
16. Hand brake.
17. Headlights and horn.
18. Starter.

6

149

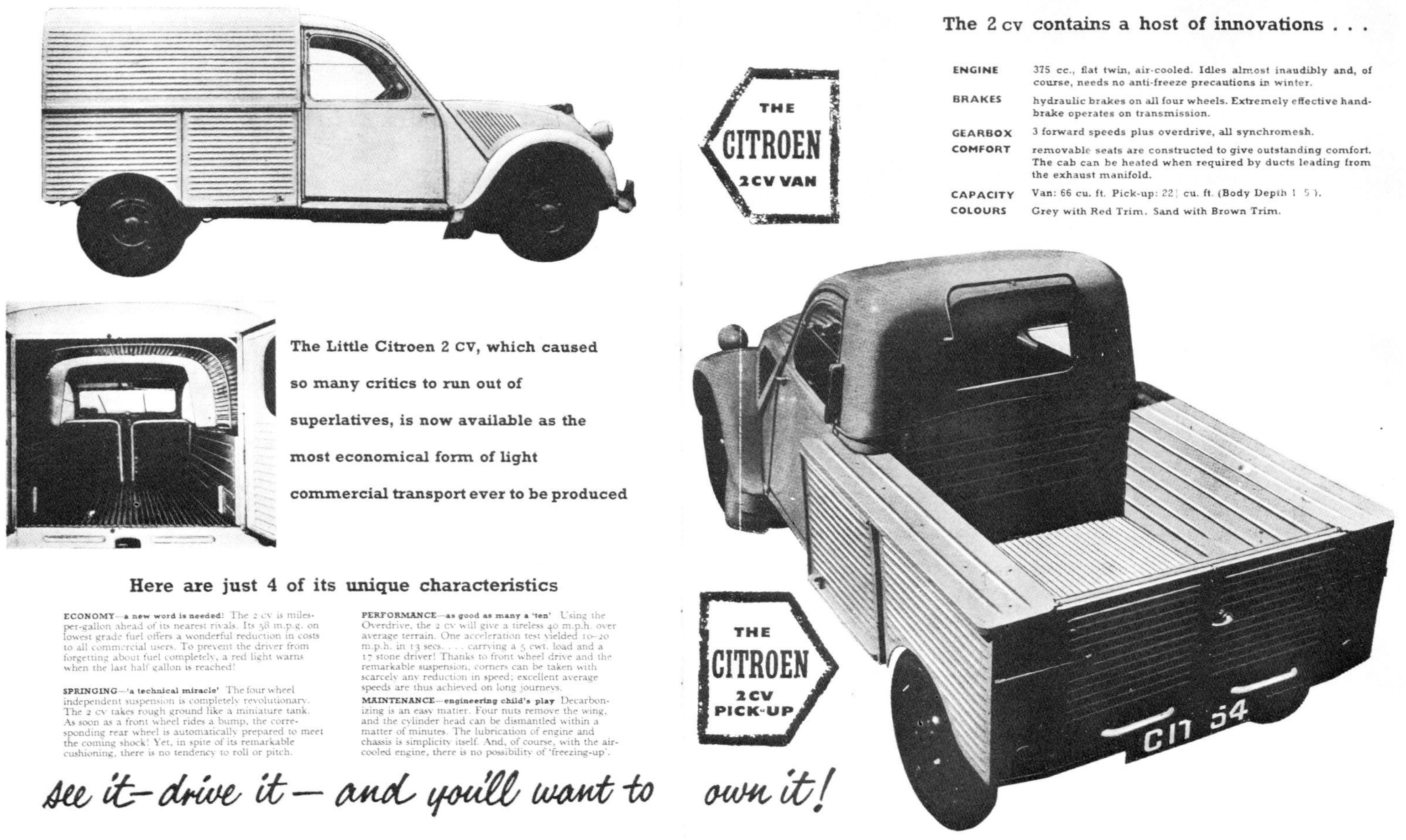

1954 Slough issued brochure for the commercial 2CVs (Citroën Car Club).

Here are just 4 of its unique characteristics

The Little Citroen 2 CV, which caused so many critics to run out of superlatives, is now available as the most economical form of light commercial transport ever to be produced

ECONOMY—A new word is needed! The 2 cv is miles-per-gallon ahead of its nearest rivals. Its 58 m.p.g. on lowest grade fuel offers a wonderful reduction in costs to all commercial users. To prevent the driver from forgetting about fuel completely, a red light warns when the last half gallon is reached.

SPRINGING—'A technical miracle'. The four wheel independent suspension is completely revolutionary. The car takes speed and rough terrain in miniature fashion. As soon as a front wheel rides a bump, the corresponding rear wheel is automatically prepared to meet the coming shock! Yet, in spite of its remarkable cushioning, there is no tendency to roll or pitch.

PERFORMANCE—as good as many a 'ten'. Using the Overdrive, the 2 CV will give a tireless 40 m.p.h. over average terrain. One acceleration test yielded 10–30 m.p.h. in 3 secs., carrying a 5 cwt. load and a 17 stone driver! Thanks to front wheel drive and the remarkable suspension, corners can be taken with scarcely any reduction in speed; excellent average speeds are thus achieved on long journeys.

MAINTENANCE—engineering child's play. Dearborn-izing is an easy matter. Four nuts remove the swing, and the cylinder head can be dismantled within a matter of minutes. The lubrication of engine and chassis is simplicity itself. And, of course, with the air-cooled engine, there is no possibility of 'freezing-up'.

see it—drive it—and you'll want to own it!

THE CITROEN 2CV VAN

THE CITROEN 2CV PICK-UP

The 2 cv contains a host of innovations....

ENGINE 375 c.c. flat twin, air-cooled. Idles almost inaudibly and, of course, needs no anti-freeze precautions in winter.

BRAKES hydraulic brakes on all four wheels. Extremely effective hand-brake operates on transmission.

GEARBOX 3 forward speeds plus overdrive, all synchromesh.

COMFORT removable seats are constructed to give outstanding comfort. The cab can be heated when required by ducts leading from the exhaust manifold.

CAPACITY Van: 66 cu. ft. Pick-up: 22 cu. ft. (Body Depth 1′5″).

COLOURS Grey with Red Trim. Sand with Brown Trim.

150

CITROËN
PRESS RELATIONS DEPT.

E. 117.320   PRESS RELEASE, NOT FOR PUBLICATION UNTIL : immediately

THE CITROËN 2 HP
"4 X 4 SAHARA"

Aware of the problems of oil prospecting in the Sahara, the CITROEN company has perfected a 2 HP model with four-wheel drive, thus adding to the car's already well-known qualities (light weight, economy, sturdiness, low maintenance cost, air-cooling, etc.) an incredible manoeuverability over sand.

The 2 HP "4 X 4", fully loaded, can go up a 45 % grade, and do it over sand (45 % represents three times the slope over the road over Izoard pass, one of the steepest highways in France).

"He who does more can also do less". First designed for the Sahara, this true mechanical workhorse will prove of tremendous use wherever road conditions are such as to present normal automotive traffic. (The car has its contribution to make to large-scale farming and ranching, public works projects, the construction of funicular railways, or of dams; it is cut out for work as liaison vehicle in underdeveloped territories, etc.). The 4 X 4 2 HP is, in fact, particularly well suited for travel over sand or other loose, unstable terrains, thanks to the following characteristics :

- low net weight (about 1400 lbs.);

- nearly equal distribution of weight over each wheel

FOR ANY FURTHER INFORMATION OR MATERIAL NEEDED, PLEASE ADDRESS ENQUIRIES TO :
CITROEN . SERVICE RELATIONS-PRESSE, 133, QUAI ANDRÉ CITROËN . PARIS XV•
TELEPHONE : VAUGIRARD 70-00 . 72-10 . 73-10 . LECOURBE 27-59 . 29-59 . EXTENSION : 2932 AND 3099

Sahara press release.

CITROËN   2

- four independently sprung wheels linked by an interacting suspension system running longitudinally on each side between front and rear wheelbase;

- outsize tyres under very low pressure;

- a relatively high-powered engine system (about 28 French HP).

TECHNICAL DETAILS

- Front and rear axles are powered by two quite independent engine assemblies (each with its own motor and transmission). There are two air-cooled horizontal bi-cylindrical engines (66x62), each with a capacity of 425 cc and each producing about 14 French HP.

- The transmissions furnish four speeds, as on the normal 2 HP.

- There is no special device to ensure synchronization of the two engines.

On the contrary, front and rear wheels can, when necessary, revolve at different speeds, thus affording increased manoeuverability over terrains presenting different surface conditions beneath each wheelbase.

When surface conditions are identical (as on the highway or over a packed earth trail), the two engines fall naturally into synchronization with each other.

- The normal 2 HP carburettors have been especially modified to prevent coughing or choking on steep climbs. Linked by cable, they are thus simultaneously commanded by the accelerator pedal.

- The two clutches are also commanded by a single pedal (again through cable linkage).

- The two transmissions are commanded simultaneously by a single shift lever. By means of a special disjunctor, the rear transmission may be shifted to neutral without affecting command over the forward transmission. In this way, the car proceed on the front engine only; there is thus provision for economizing petrol consumption over easy surfaces.

CITROËN   3

- 8 X 31 conical coupling

- Reinforced "overseas-type" chassis with the underside of both engines protected by skis, a system which allows deep ruts to be crossed without danger to the car.

Tubular front and rear bumpers (At both front and rear, the vehicle can be lifted and released by hand from mud or any other obstacle).

- Since the rear of this car is likely to bear more weight than the normal 2 HP, the frame has been built to lie in a completely horizontal plane, so that the whole portion of the chassis lying ahead of the forward axle is raised, the car thus acquiring greater manoeuverability over rough terrain.

- The brakes, located at the working ends of forward and rear transmissions, have been well protected against the intrusion of mud or dust.

- The car utilizes "X"-type tyres, most suitable for driving over sand, thanks to treads that cannot lose their shape. These tyres are, moreover, very oversized. The 155x400 "X"-type tyres is capable of supporting 1750 lbs. per axle, whereas the load weight per axle on the 2 HP "4 X 4 Sahara" does nor overstep a maximum of 1034 lbs. (704 lbs. empty). Tyre pressure can, without risk, be reduced to 9 1/2 lbs./sq.in., a great advantage over bad surfaces. The same pressure can be maintained while travelling, so that continual bleeding and refilling of the tyres are avoided. The spare tyre is located on the bonnet.

PERFORMANCE : With its full load (four adults) the car can be driven over any sort of surface and can climb up slopes of about 45 %.

Speed over the highway : more than 60 m.p.h.

Petrol consumption : 31 miles per gallon on the highway;
23 to 25 miles per gallon over other surfaces.

Specifications

Type AZ, 2 CV (12 BHP at 3,500 rpm)—Four stroke, 425 c.c., (26 cu.in.) flat-twin engine (removable cylinders)—Air cooling : no trouble with freezing or boiling—Three forward speeds, plus overdrive, all synchronized, and one reverse—Clutch fitted with an auxiliary centrifugal control—Hydraulic brakes on the four wheels.

Electrical equipment : road lighting adjustable according to load, while running. Tyres : Michelin 135 × 400.

FOR INFORMATION AND DEMONSTRATION, PLEASE APPLY TO

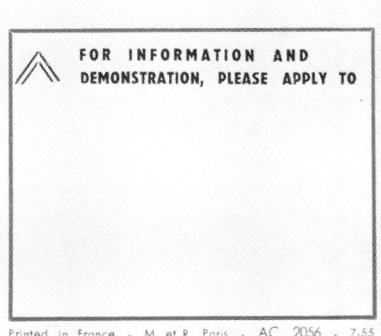

Printed in France - M. et R. Paris - AC. 2056 - 7-55

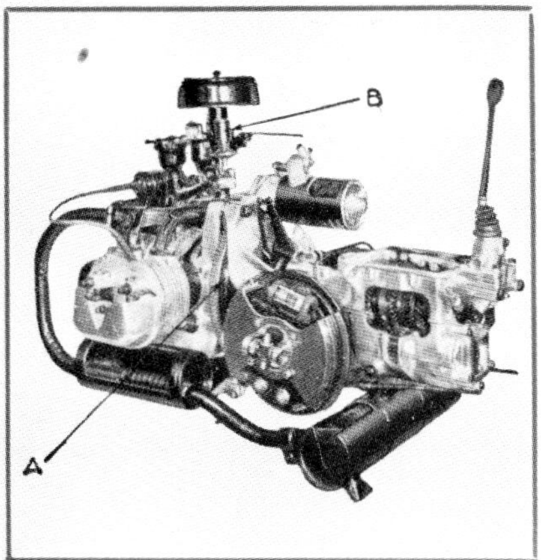

The 2 CV engine (section)
A - Clutch   B - Idling retarding device

Comforta[ble]

There is ample accomodation for four peop[le] seat comfortably and cross their legs or st[retch] them. The soft seats and special susper[sion] system definitely absorb all road shocks.

The front seats are adjustable; both r[ear] front seats are easily removable so that th[ey] be used, when camping for instance, a[s] chairs.

Very efficient heating through two hot air v[ents]

Easy to handle

The clutch with its auxiliary centrifugal control makes town driving particularly easy, when one has endlessly to slow down, stop and start again; the only thing to do is to accelerate more or less without having to bother with the clutch pedal or the gear lever.

Traditional road holding ability of front-wheel drive cars. Very powerful brakes.

Amazing suspension added to front-wheel drive permits long journeys without fatigue and in perfect safety even on slippery and winding roads.

Overall
Overall
Overall h[eight]

1955 British sales brochure.

CITROËN

2 CV

Type AZ - 425 c.c., (26 cu. in.)

and Strong

Excellent adjustable ventilation by means of progressive opening of the windshield flap. Besides its high degree of comfort, the car, which can be partially or totally uncovered, offers many possibilities for carrying various articles.
The mechanical components of the 2 CV are generously designed. The quality of metals, the precision and severity of inspection make it a car worthy of the best Citroën technique. The 2 CV is built to last.

An unusually roomy luggage compartment

Economical

The low operating cost of the 2 CV may be best appreciated when using and maintaining it : about 55 miles per Imperial gallon; crankcase capacity : only 3.5 pints; four grease fittings only.

Good average speeds

38 to 40 miles per hour average speed on easy roads with four people and a hundredweight of luggage. On level, on overdrive, you can keep up 47 mph without difficulty. Uphill, the 2 CV climbs on steadily. It can negociate all European mountain passes, without overheating.

ledroit dans le même anno... risé plus d'essence qu'il n'en faut.

Peut-être les compagnies de distribution prélèvent-elles des bénéfices exagérés? Qu'on en juge. Leur marge brute s'établit en France à 3,2% du prix de vente. Ce n'est pas exorbitant pour assurer le ravitaillement quotidien de toutes les citernes d'essence. Le bénéfice brut des stations-service est parfaitement raisonnable; il est fixé à 3 %.

A la pompe, le litre d'essence, tous frais payés, tout bénéfice encaissé, ne coûte pas plus de 25,70 F. Si nous payons 99 F, c'est que l'Etat prélève au passage 73,30 F de taxes et d'impôts divers.

Au mois d'août dernier, le litre d'essence a encore été majoré de 1 F. Ce n'est pas grand-chose; peu de chose, dira-t-on; mais étant donné qu'en France la fiscalité est en sens unique, les hausses ne font que s'accumuler et, aujourd'hui, l'automobiliste ne peut plus mettre réellement qu'un quart d'essence; les trois autres quarts étant occupés par l'impôt.

Celui qui, pour son travail, a réellement besoin d'une voiture doit y regarder à deux fois avant de faire des kilomètres. En France, où le prix de l'essence est exceptionnellement élevé, le succès de la 2 CV est dû en grande partie à la faiblesse de sa consommation.

Terminons enfin par le dernier de ces excellents tests. A la date de ces lignes, la revue de consommation « Mobil Economy Run 1959 », de Copenhague, n'a pas encore livré les résultats de son concours qui n'en reste pas moins une victoire sans précédent pour

HONY TEST D'AVRIL
en tête du classement par consommation: Trois 2 CV ont occupé les 3 premières places au Classement des 37 participants (classés, car il y avait 52 partants) qui avait pour but les tests de consommation. La très faible consommation des 2 CV démontre la sobriété du moteur bicylindre Citroën. Dans un pays où la circulation automobile est considérablement alourdi par les taxes fiscales, la sobriété devient facteur économique numéro un.

LA 2 CV arrivent en tête du classement par consommation: Trois 2 CV ont couru sur 2.000 km de routes avec une consommation de 4,10 litres. C'est M. Choterre encore, fanatique des concours de consommation et de la 2 CV, qui, avec sa Citroën Noire à Copenhague, n'a obtenu qu'une consommation que 3,75 litres aux 100 km.

M. Choterre a réalisé la consommation de 3 litres 75 aux 100 km (Avril 1959).

Photo junior (Nice)

M. Zemeiron a réalisé la consommation de 3 litres 81 aux 100 km (Juin 1939).

En 1958, elle a importé 28 millions de tonnes de pétrole brut (et 1,7 million de tonnes de produits finis). La production nationale (de 1,4 million de tonnes, on a foré 765.000 m de terre et investi 262 milliards de francs. L'industrie pétrolière française emploie 70.000 personnes. Sans elle, il n'y aurait plus d'autos, plus de motos, plus de bitume sur les routes, plus de mazout dans les chaudières, plus de carburant dans les fours, plus d'huile pour les machines, etc.

Aujourd'hui, la France produit près de cinq fois plus d'huile et consomme dix fois plus de pétrole ultra-moderne. En 1958, en imports 28 millions de T

U.S.A.	350 millions de T
Venezuela	115
U.R.S.S.	65
Koweït	50, 55
Arabie	40
France	—

(voir page 4)

Vous aussi profitez de L'ÉPARGNE 2 CV

L'AVENIR DES TRANSPORTS SAHARIENS

De tout temps l'homme a caressé le rêve de franchir les déserts — et en particulier du Sahara. Mais les vents qui souffient avec une extrême violence déplacent continuellement cette infrastructure dépasse aucunes prévisions raisonnables d'un amortissement.

Entre temps le développement du transport aérien a fait perdre une partie de l'intérêt d'une installation de chemin de fer qui permet aucun rayonnement en dehors de son itinéraire: pour son attérissement comme pour le transport les charges précieuses peu volumineuses. Au surplus, un transcontinental comme le rail aura toujours besoin d'un moyen de transport terrestre capable de faire du porte à porte, c'est-à-dire dans le cas plus scabreux allant de la tête onduleuse au reg en passant par la hamada, il faut donc recourir à des véhicules automobiles tout terrain.

Dans ce domaine il est certain que la première traversée du Sahara réalisée en 1923 par la mission Citroën avec des autochenilles ouvrait la seule voie possible à la gare de transport de ce genre. La Croisière Noire en 1924 couronnait les espérances que l'on pouvait fonder sur l'automobilisme saharien.

Les voitures Citroën (notre mar-que) et Panhard s'édiguaient les trois premières places du Classement classeme 3,81 litres aux 100 km, soit moins

Il faut faire une remarque au sujet du classement des 2 CV dans des tests de consommation. La très faible consommation de la 2 CV résulte non de son rendement particulier mais de l'absolue contrainte que s'impose le constructeur de ne pas lâcher la conception d'un moteur à 2 CV fiscales. L'indice a établi sur le nombre de tonnes kilométriques au litre est considéré comme on y aurait pu le supposer comme le premier plan destinées à les établir dans le désert. Il restait évidemment bien des progrès à réaliser dans la construction de véhicules sahariens: d'autre part grâce à l'édification, sur certains axes de choix, d'un réseau routier utilisant les moyens les plus modernes actuellement connus qui permettent de faire des travaux publics, tout fait prévoir sans doute que le jour viendra sans doute un renouveau des essais de la Traversée du Sahara, grâce à la mise en marche de gigantesques chantiers, l'aménagement et l'entretien des pistes, la pose des oléoducs, la 2 CV étant déjà entre les travaux de liaison quotidiens entre les chantiers et les habitations.

Parmi ces véhicules de liaison, camionnettes et tracteurs des grands constructeurs ont rivalisé de puissance d'audace ou de l'économie. Citroën chaussés les Sahara, 4 x 4 à 6 roues motrices, Panhard, 108 et le camion Citroën 76 ch type 46 Diesel à 4 roues motrices. On peut se demander si la la 2 CV, dans ce domaine, Sahara à 4 ou 6 roues motrices, ne sera pas le plus efficace, la 4 CV type

concluants, à subi avec le succès que l'on sait les épreuves du sable désertique et, même récemment, un record mondial d'écon-nomique avant été battu dans ce terrain sablonneux, ce qui constitue un terrain sablonneux dans son domaine: la 2 CV étant désignée prédestinée à devenir petit 4 x 4 lui permet d'affron-ter les rampes de 40% en tous terrains, l'adhérence de la voiture passe-partout.

La 2 CV type 4 x 4 lige agrément ses deux moteurs grâce au grand volume du coffre arrière.

La voiture saharienne Citroën (4 x 4 à 2 essieux moteurs) à l'essai au pied du pic Laperrine (Haggar) (Numéro spécial Sahara).

Le camion Citroën 5,5 tonnes à 4 roues motrices (Diesel type 4 x 4)

Le « Scarabée d'or » (Première Traversée du Sahara en automobile en 1923)

Many thanks to David Conway for allowing us access to this 1959 copy of Le Citroën.

LE CITROËN

3 litres 81 aux 100 km (MOBIL ECONOMY RUN 1959)

ÉDITION SPÉCIALE RÉSERVÉE AUX PROPRIÉTAIRES ET FUTURS PROPRIÉTAIRES DE 2 CV

4ᵉ TRIMESTRE 1959

RÉDACTION-ADMINISTRATION : 117 à 167, QUAI ANDRÉ CITROËN, PARIS (XVᵉ)
FEUILLE PUBLICITAIRE ÉDITÉE PAR LA SOCIÉTÉ ANONYME ANDRÉ CITROËN (CAPITAL SOCIAL DE 17.080 MILLIONS DE FRANCS)

NOËL 1959

Joyeuses fêtes — bonne année !

TRANSPORTS CHERS

VIE CHÈRE

TOUT ce que nous achetons pour notre vie quotidienne, il a bien fallu que des autos le transportent sur les marchés, dans les magasins ou à domicile. Le prix de ces transports est évidemment répercuté sur celui des marchandises.

Les transports de distribution et le porte-à-porte se font en auto. Quand l'essence augmente, tout augmente. L'essence chère fait la vie chère.

L'AUTOMOBILISTE français jouit d'un privilège peu glorieux : celui de payer l'essence la plus chère du monde. A ce grand ennemi, il possède heureusement un grand remède, car c'est en France aussi que l'on construit la voiture 4 places-4 portes la plus économique de la 2 à 6 litres à pleine charge. En fait, nombreux sont les utilisateurs qui reconnaissent consommer moins.

Dans les concours de consommation organisés chaque année par les grandes sociétés pétrolières, la 2 CV prouve qu'elle sait consommer, quand elle est bien conduite, à peine plus qu'une grosse moto.

Ainsi, au **Mobilgas Economy Run** 1958 d'Angleterre, la 2 CV CITROËN, 1ʳᵉ de la catégorie jusqu'à 1.000 cm³, n'avait consommé, au cours d'un itinéraire de 1842 km, que **4,08 litres aux 100 km**.

Deux mois après, se courait la

RECORDS 2 CV
aux concours de consommation

LA FRANCE PUISSANCE PÉTROLIÈRE

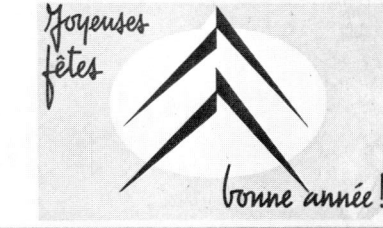

EN attendant que l'énergie atomique soit le moteur du monde de demain, le pétrole reste encore la première source d'énergie du XXᵉ siècle. Son rôle s'accroît d'année en année. Il y a vingt ans, l'essence et le gas-oil ne fournissaient qu'une faible part de l'énergie industrielle française. Les produits pétroliers servent presque exclusivement à l'alimentation des moteurs de véhicules. Aujourd'hui, à peu près la cinquième partie de l'énergie est fournie en France par les produits pétroliers. Aux États-Unis les pétroliers, mazout et gaz de pétrole sont les principales sources d'énergie.

Vers 1930, au moment où la France, comme les pays producteurs d'automobiles du monde, cherchait à accroître le...

Quant aux produits finis, on en a acheté en U.R.S.S., aux États-Unis, en Roumanie, etc.

Tout peut changer avec le pétrole saharien. Car si l'on devait que 1,5 million de tonnes, en 1960 la production sera déjà au minimum de **12 millions de tonnes.**

Le 10 novembre dernier, premier anniversaire d'Hassi-Messaoud a coulé à Bougie, point terminal du pipe-line. Bientôt le premier pétrolier chargera les premières tonnes de brut à destination de la métropole.

En 1961 ce seront 22 millions de tonnes, 29 en 1962, 35 en 1963, 50 à 55 millions en 1965. Dans ces conditions, les bassins de...

APPENDIX V
ONE ENTHUSIAST'S VIEW

2cv's are.....light to push.......

COMBATANTS TAKE UP OPPOSING positions for the annual M.O.T.!

CITROEN ADAPTATION PART NO 8302 FOR SERIOUS GAME FISHING

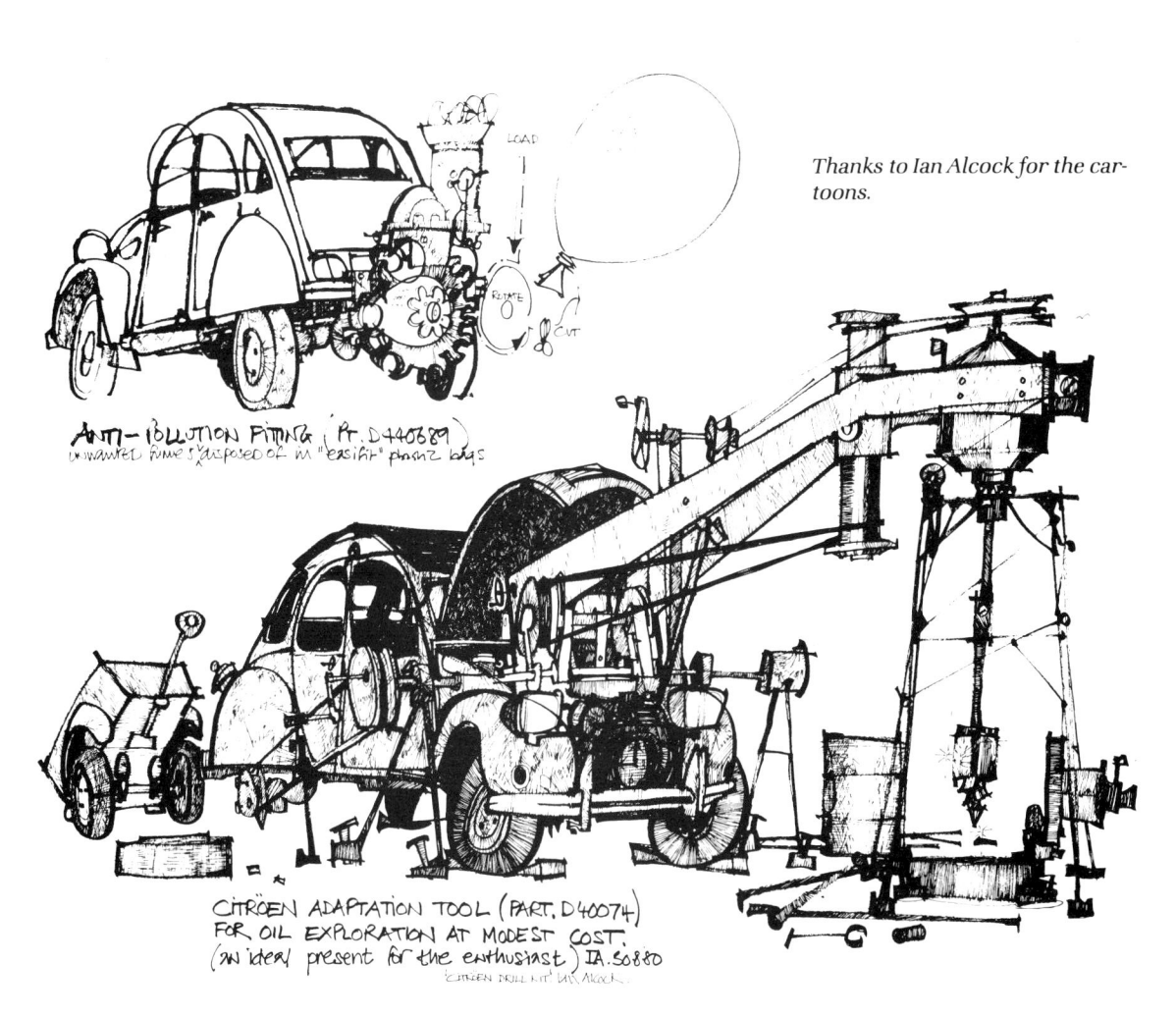

ANTI-POLLUTION FITTING (Pt. D40689)
unwanted fumes disposed of in "easifit" plastic bags

Thanks to Ian Alcock for the cartoons.

CITROEN ADAPTATION TOOL (PART. D40074)
FOR OIL EXPLORATION AT MODEST COST.
(an ideal present for the enthusiast) IA.50880
'CITROEN DRILL KIT' IAN ALCOCK

CITROËN KIT ANTI-THEFT
A.
B
C
D
BOING!
Zut!
SACRÉ BLEU!!!
CITROËN 2CV/DYANE
ANTI-THEFT DEVICE
PART NO. 1A·184D.

Thank you P.J.B.